Company Tax Reform
in the
European Union

COMPANY TAX REFORM
IN THE
EUROPEAN UNION

GUIDANCE FROM THE UNITED STATES AND CANADA
ON IMPLEMENTING
FORMULARY APPORTIONMENT IN THE EU

JOANN MARTENS-WEINER

 Springer

Library of Congress Control Number: 2005933745
ISBN-10: 0-387-29424-4   e-ISBN 0-387-29487-2
ISBN-13: 978-0387-29424-7

Printed on acid-free paper.

Printed in the United States of America.

9 8 7 6 5 4 3 2 1

springeronline.com

To Josh, Stephen, and Naomi

CONTENTS

List of Tables ix

Foreword
By Joseph H. Guttentag xi

Preface xv

Acknowledgments xvii

1. Company Tax Reform and Formulary Apportionment in the
   European Union 1

2. The Landscape for EU Company Tax Reform 17

3. Formulary Apportionment in the European Union 33

4. The Apportionment Formula 47

5. Nexus, The Tax Base and the Taxable Unit 61

6. Tax Administration, Compliance and Tax Planning 77

7. Economic Analysis of Formulary Apportionment 89

8. Conclusion: Implementing Formulary Apportionment in the
   European Union 105

   Bibliography 109

   Index 117

LIST OF TABLES

Table 1   Corporate income tax rates in the EU-15 and in the new EU Member States, selected years

Table 2   Domestic and cross-border loss offsetting in the EU Member States, 2005

Table 3   Illustration of cross-border income shifting

Table 4   Selected European Court of Justice direct tax cases

Table 5   Income distribution under formulary apportionment

Table 6   Distribution of employees across the EU Member States, Q2-2002

Table 7   Illustration of factor and income distribution under apportionment for Unilever

Table 8   Illustration of state apportionment factors

Table 9   Illustration of apportionment formula calculation in Canada

Table 10   Computation of state taxable income for multistate corporation

Table 11   Selected state policies

Table 12   State apportionment tax rates, 2005

Table 13   Calculations of EU formulary apportionment tax rates under different capital factor weights

Box 1   Derivation of marginal effective tax rates under formulary apportionment

FOREWORD

Having spent almost fifty years of my life defending the separate accounting, arm's length pricing method, I have to admit that I was somewhat surprised to be asked to contribute to a book suggesting that the European Union might do well to consider adopting a formulary approach to deal with the taxation of inter and intra company transactions.

I was even more surprised to see the invitation coming from Ms. Joann Weiner an ardent co-defender of arm's length pricing and my strong right arm in that regard while we both served in the U.S. Treasury Department in the mid '90s. The book gives Ms Weiner the opportunity to comment frankly from an insider's perspective of the many admitted problems of the arm's length system which could be avoided by a formulary approach.

Ms. Weiner brings to this project a thorough expert knowledge of the benefits and shortfalls of each of the systems she discusses – separate accounting v. formulary apportionment. Who better to decide to give qualified support to formulary than someone who organized a U.S. Treasury conference to defend arm's length pricing against a Congressional challenge in favor of formulary apportionment.

The recommendations of the EU Commission will require substantial study and will undoubtedly go through many permutations and engender many responses and much support as well as criticism. Ms Weiner makes a significant contribution to this major project by analysis and demonstration of formulary systems in sub-national jurisdictions in the United States and Canada. The economic and legal systems of the United States and Canada bear some significant similarity to those of the EU. However there are other factors which caution us when attempting to replicate such systems in the EU. There is a substantial difference with respect to the sovereign powers of the EU with relation to its members, compared with those of the United States and Canada. The tax rates affected by such a system in the EU would be generally higher than those affected in the U.S. and Canada thereby making any system, separate accounting or formulary apportionment, and its advantages or disadvantages more important in the EU.

The book does not claim that formulary apportionment is a flawless system. Rather, the book shows that, when constructed properly --- meaning designing a system that addresses the problems that arise in the existing systems in the U.S. states and Canadian provinces --- formulary apportionment is a viable replacement for separate accounting in the European Union.

Readers frustrated by having to deal with separate accounting tax problems of multi-nationals need to be cautioned that they should not look here for a proposal to drop separate accounting world-wide in favor of formulary apportionment. The EU proposal envisages adoption of a common tax base and a common apportionment method by member states. EU criteria establish certain economic standards for admittance, there is a Monetary Union although all members do not belong, and a single market is the cornerstone of the EU. In my opinion, it is unlikely that the conditions which suggest the use of formulary apportionment within the EU will exist worldwide.

Ms Weiner's major contribution to this ongoing discussion must be her analysis, taking up over half of her book, of how formulary apportionment works in practice using, as noted, the sub-national U.S. and Canada examples. About one-half of the OECD member countries are EU members and they have been bombarded over the past fifty years as to the desirability of the arm's length pricing methodology. For those who wish to evaluate formulary apportionment from a new perspective, this book provides all the necessary tools --- from an analysis of how to design an apportionment formula to a discussion of how to prepare a tax form --- to make that evaluation.

Readers who are interested in the mechanics of how formulary apportionment operates will appreciate the detailed examples provided in chapter 3. Of course, the real world is more complicated than the world on paper, but these examples illustrate the simplicity of using a formula to distribute income across various EU Member States. Choosing apportionment factors wisely, as explained in chapter 4, can greatly reduce the potential investment distortions caused by tax rate differences.

Chapter 5 shows that the international community already deals with many issues that arise when a company does business in more than one taxing jurisdiction. For example, when does a non-resident have a taxable connection? Does it occur only when it has a "permanent establishment" or may it occur when it has an "economic presence?" Should countries continue to make the distinction between how they treat business profits and how they treat individual items of income, such as dividends, royalties, and capital gains? How should the taxable unit be defined? These questions must be addressed before moving to formulary apportionment, but they should not impede the decision to make such a move.

The Commission's Study only touched on tax administration issues. For EU tax authorities, Chapter 6 provides a valuable discussion of how to administer a "multistate" EU tax system --- it does not require developing an EU tax organization. This chapter also confronts the tax planning issue head on. Multistate and multinational companies can, and will, find tax planning opportunities. The challenge for EU tax authorities is to find effective ways to address these opportunities without creating a tax compliance cure that is worse than the tax planning disease. Chapter 6 provides food for thought for those who see formulary apportionment with combined reporting as nothing but a taxpayer's nightmare.

Finally, chapter 7 provides reassuring evidence for those who fear that formulary apportionment will restrict EU Member State tax sovereignty. Even if Member States adopt a common formula and common tax base, they can still encourage additional investment and employment through setting competitive tax rates.

This work has tremendous value, but it does not pretend to cover the multitude of issues generated by the European Commission Report. Others will I am sure be writing in depth of the interaction of the adoption of an internal formulary method on the pervasive worldwide arm's length method, whether a formulary system should be applied worldwide by EU members, the effect of a formulary system in the EU on complying with arm's length systems elsewhere and numerous other issues.

The author has the advantage of her training and experience in dealing with the relevant tax systems in North America and also experience with current problems from her vantage point in Brussels through her contribution to the Ruding Committee and recent work for the European Commission studying the future shape of EU tax systems. As an American living and working in Brussels, the author provides a unique insight into how the U.S. system may work in the European Union.

The book reflects the expertise of a well-qualified economist and will be a valuable tool for the European Commission and staff, the member countries who would change their tax systems, and the multi-nationals affected by such changes.

Joseph H. Guttentag
Deputy Assistant Secretary (International Tax Affairs)
U.S. Department of the Treasury
(Retired)

South Bristol, Maine
September 15, 2005

PREFACE

The European Commission has set forth a new strategy for taxing multinational enterprises that would simplify tax compliance and reduce cross-border investment barriers. The Commission proposes allowing EU multinational enterprises to compute a common EU tax base using a single set of tax rules at the EU level and then to distribute this tax base across the individual Member States using an agreed common "apportionment mechanism." Consistent with preserving Member State sovereignty in direct tax matters, the individual Member States would apply the local tax rate to their share of the EU tax base.

The existence of separate EU Member State tax systems is the heart of the company tax problem in the EU, and European Union policy makers are growing to appreciate the relative success of the U.S. and Canadian formulary apportionment systems in addressing this problem. The European Commission's proposal creates an opportune time to undertake an-depth evaluation of the benefits and drawbacks of using formulary apportionment to distribute a common tax base across the EU Member States.

This book pursues three main objectives. First, it sets the context for EU company tax reform by identifying some difficulties that arise when using separate accounting as the method for taxing EU multinationals in the Internal Market. It also seeks to dispel any latent concerns over the merits of using formulary apportionment in the EU.

The book's second objective is to guide EU policy makers and businesses through the basic contours of a potential EU formulary apportionment system. It pursues this objective by presenting a range of examples on how formulary apportionment works, drawing from European Union data. It also uses practical examples from the U.S. and Canada to illustrate how to implement formulary apportionment and to identify some technical and administrative issues that must be resolved when implementing the new method.

The book's final objective is to evaluate how the empirical and theoretical evidence may affect the decision to move to formulary apportionment. The empirical evidence demonstrates that preserving the ability to set local tax rates, preserves the EU Member States' ability to create a competitive business environment. The theoretical evidence is a bit less conclusive: formulary apportionment has an ambiguous effect on tax competition relative to separate accounting.

The book's over-riding objective is to create a "level analytical field" between separate accounting and formulary apportionment. With such a starting point, EU policymakers have the fundamental tools necessary to help decide whether to move to formulary apportionment in the European Union.

ACKNOWLEDGMENTS

The generous help of many friends and colleagues has greatly improved the quality and content of this book. I thank Reuven Avi-Yonah, Charles E. McLure, Jr., Lillian Mills, Kelly Edmiston, Sanjay Gupta, Jack Mintz, and Robert Brown for their help shaping the contours of this book. I thank Benjamin F. Miller, James W. Wetzler, Stella Raventós-Calvo, Andreas Wagener, Silvia Giannini, Friedrich Roedler, Hugh Ault, Valerie Amerkhail, Jacques Sasseville, Susan Nelson, Michael Durst, Matthias Mors and Richard Weiner for their assistance in refining the present text. I thank Richard especially for his patience, kindness, and support through this long process. I especially thank Emil Sunley, Timothy J. Goodspeed, Joseph Guttentag, Marcel Gérard, and Albert Rädler for their detailed comments on the full text. I especially thank Walter Hellerstein for his careful attention to the content of this book and for his invaluable suggestions concerning the direction and analysis contained in this book. I am grateful for all of the gracious and kind assistance that so many people have offered to me, and I thank you all for your help in making this book possible.

Chapter 1

COMPANY TAX REFORM AND FORMULARY APPORTIONMENT IN THE EUROPEAN UNION

1.1 THE EUROPEAN COMMISSION'S COMPANY TAX STRATEGY

The European Commission has presented a comprehensive company tax strategy that would fundamentally restructure how multinational enterprises are taxed in the European Union.[1] The Commission reasons that EU multinational enterprises should be able to calculate a consolidated tax base at the EU-level using a single set of tax rules. In addition, EU Member States should be able to continue to set the rate of tax to apply to their portion of EU profits. Adopting a system of consolidated base taxation with formulary apportionment allows the Commission to achieve its goals in a single stroke.

The Commission's strategy simplifies tax compliance and removes the tax obstacles to cross-border investment created by the twenty-five separate company tax systems in the European Union. The Commission Study (2002) charges that certain tax obstacles "undermine the international competitiveness of European companies and waste resources" and are incompatible with the Single Market. Many factors affect the competitiveness of EU multinational enterprises, but requiring them to apply twenty-five different sets of tax rules to compute and then to distribute their profits across the Member States does not improve their competitiveness.

The European Commission's strategy is a break from tradition in company taxation in the European Union. Formulary apportionment --- the method of using a formula to distribute a multinational enterprise's profits across jurisdictions --- is a new approach for allocating income across the European Union.[2] The traditional method --- separate accounting with arm's length pricing --- requires a multinational enterprise to calculate a separate tax base in each Member State as if each entity within the affiliated group were an independent entity operating at arm's length.

Under separate accounting with arm's length pricing, a multinational enterprise establishes a transfer price for each cross-border transfer of goods, services, and intangibles with its related affiliates on an "arm's length" basis.[3] Under formulary apportionment, by contrast, the multinational enterprise apportions its total profits across locations based on the share of its total business activity (e.g., demonstrated by its tangible property, payroll expenses, and sales revenues) in each location. Thus, consolidated base taxation with formulary apportionment largely eliminates the need for companies to find arm's length transfer prices --- the "Achilles heel of separate accounting" --- for cross-border transactions with controlled affiliates within the European Union.[4]

Using a formula to distribute profits across *international* borders is a new method not only for the European Union on the whole, but also for most EU Member States. Although some European nations used formulary methods in the early 20th century and many use formulae for other purposes, nations have rarely used formulary apportionment to distribute profits across international borders.[5]

Formulary apportionment, however, is not a new method for distributing profits across sub-national borders. The U.S. states and Canadian provinces have used formulary apportionment for more than half a century as the principal method to distribute company profits across locations for taxation at the respective state and provincial levels.

The European Union can obtain valuable guidance from examining how the U.S. states and Canadian provinces have resolved the economic, political and technical aspects of using formulary apportionment to distribute profits across taxing borders. As the Commission Study (2002) points out, "The U.S. and Canadian examples illustrate that formulary apportionment can work . . . and provide a valuable source of experience and precedent for Member States should they choose to pursue this route."

EU multinational businesses generally agree with the Commission's strategy.[6] The Union of Industrial and Employers' Confederations in Europe (UNICE), a federation representing the views of European industry, supports the Commission's tax strategy and views the new approach as a logical development for the European Union. As UNICE (2000) notes, the tax history in the United States and Canada shows that they "adopted systems which address these obstacles [multiple tax systems, no loss offsetting, transfer pricing] by having a common taxable base but which simultaneously maintain flexibility by leaving the decision on tax rates to the different jurisdictions."[7]

The European Union is poised to embark on a new direction in company taxation.[8] To provide guidance in this endeavor, this book describes the landscape for company tax reform in the European Union and how formulary apportionment fits into that landscape. The book draws extensively from experiences in the U.S. states and Canadian provinces to illustrate how formulary apportionment works.[9]

The book discusses practical issues concerning the fundamental elements of a formulary apportionment system — the formula, the tax base, and the taxable group — and how formulary apportionment may affect the investment and employment decisions of multinational enterprises in the European Union. It addresses administrative and compliance issues as well as some tax planning opportunities that arise and how tax authorities have responded to those opportunities. It also discusses the implications of recent theoretical research on how formulary apportionment may affect tax competition in the European Union. It concludes with final thoughts on introducing formulary apportionment in the European Union.

To provide background to the analysis, the next section briefly examines the current method for taxing multinational enterprises in the European Union.[10] The remainder of the chapter discusses the historical view of formulary apportionment in the European Union and how EU governments and businesses came to view formulary apportionment in a favorable light.

1.2   MULTINATIONAL TAXATION IN THE EUROPEAN UNION

Separate accounting has a long history in Europe and around the world. The international community adopted the separate accounting, independent enterprise method in the early 20th century as the agreed method to determine the amount of income a multinational enterprise earned in each country. The international community considered the possibility of adopting formulary apportionment, but concluded that since the tax, economic, and legal barriers surrounding nations led multinational enterprises to calculate their profits on a separate entity basis, it made sense for countries to adopt a tax system that also treated enterprises on a separate entity basis.[11]

Under current business practices, multinational enterprises generally operate outside their home markets through subsidiaries. These subsidiaries must report their income and be taxed according to the laws of the countries in which they are located, so they must use separate entity accounting, and must apply the arm's length principle in establishing transfer prices for transactions with affiliates.

The method of separate entity accounting under the arm's length principle respects the separate legal status of affiliates within a multinational enterprise (MNE) and treats each related entity as if it operated as an independent entity at arm's length. The basic idea underlying the arm's length principle is relatively simple. Enterprises should set the prices for internal transfers among controlled entities in the same manner that enterprises operating independently, or at "arm's length," set prices on the market.

Separate accounting under the arm's length principle has many advantages. First, it aims to place integrated and independent companies on the same tax footing. As the OECD (1995) notes, proper application of the arm's length pricing principle should eliminate any special conditions that may affect the level of profits.

OECD member countries have chosen the arm's length principle since it "provides broad parity of tax treatment for MNEs and independent enterprises," thus eliminating any tax advantages or disadvantages that might accrue solely from the organizational form of the enterprise.[12] An integrated enterprise should not be able to gain tax advantages through manipulating its internal transfer prices. This notion of treating associated and independent enterprises on the same tax basis has strong appeal.

An important reason to apply separate accounting under the arm's length principle is that the international community has reached near consensus to use this method to distribute multinational profits across countries. This agreement exists not only in international practice, but also in Model tax treaties and in the worldwide network of bilateral income tax treaties. The OECD Model Income Tax Convention, for example, incorporates this principle in Article 9 (Associated Enterprises) and in Article 7 (Business Profits).

Reaching consensus is essential to minimize the risk of double taxation and to alleviate double taxation when it does arise. The broad acceptance of this method as the international norm provide a strong justification for its continued use at the international level.

1.3   A NEW METHOD FOR TAXING COMPANIES IN THE EUROPEAN UNION

Despite these advantages, however, there are good reasons to move away from this method, especially within the European Union. Much of the support for separate entity accounting diminishes when considering the taxation of enterprises within an economically integrated area. For example, if EU enterprises operate at the EU level, why should they continue to treat these enterprises as if they were separate entities and calculate their profits on a transaction-by-transaction basis for Member State tax purposes? If EU enterprises are allowed to compute a common EU-level tax base, does it make sense to require them to re-calculate the tax base on a separate entity basis solely for Member State tax purposes?

The European Commission (2002, 2003a) provides a clear response to these fundamental questions. If EU companies have integrated their operations at the EU level, then they should be taxed on their EU profits at the EU level. For tax purposes, the best response to these business developments is to treat enterprises doing business across the European Union as integrated EU enterprises rather than, for example, as separate Belgian, French, or German companies operating as independent entities in individual Member States. However, to preserve Belgian, French, and German tax sovereignty, these EU-level profits must be distributed to the Member States for taxation at locally determined rates. The answer to the second question then depends on how that distribution is made.

EU Member States could continue with the traditional approach and apply source of income and expense rules to distribute the combined EU-level tax base across related entities in the various Member States.[13] Doing so requires the taxpayer first to identify the type of income and determine its geographic source and then to apply various accounting principles or similar source of income and expense rules to match expenses to that gross income.[14]

Alternatively, Member States could adopt a new approach and distribute the EU tax base across the Member States using a simple formula based on where the taxpayer conducts its business. This process avoids re-introducing the transfer pricing burdens that the creation of a consolidated tax base eliminates.

EU businesses are increasingly critical of the process of establishing transfer prices for tax purposes. They explain that EU companies "have to determine what prices could be regarded as arm's length, to find comparables, put the related documentation together, defend these prices, incur the related compliance costs and run the risk of double taxation, whereas transfer prices within Europe are not even relevant from a business point of view."[15] The centralization of operations at the EU-level, the growth of cross-border intra-firm transactions, and the increasing importance of transfers of intangibles for which comparable transactions do not exist, call into question the wisdom of continuing to allocate income across the European Union under separate accounting and the arm's length principle.

1.4 OBSTACLES ON THE ROAD TO FORMULARY APPORTIONMENT

Even with strong support from EU businesses, the European Commission faces an uphill struggle in implementing its comprehensive strategy. In addition to convincing Member States of the importance of a common EU-level tax base, the European Commission must also convince the Member States of the advantages of using formulary apportionment as the mechanism to distribute that common tax base across the European Union.

The European Commission has tried many times to promote a common company tax system in the EU Member States.[16] The Commission's most recent effort at company tax reform occurred in 1990, when it released new guidelines on company taxation and established a committee of independent tax experts, which became known as the Ruding Committee, to take a "fresh start" in evaluating company taxation in the European Union.

The Ruding Committee examined various forms of company tax systems --- split rate, imputation, classical --- that would allow the European Community to reap the full benefits of the Single Market, but it did not recommend any specific system.[17] Furthermore, although the Ruding Report includes annexes discussing the formulary methods in Canada, Switzerland, and the United States, the Ruding Committee firmly rejected formulary apportionment.[18]

The reasons for this sound rejection are not clear, but they may be related to the perception that formulary apportionment inappropriately taxes income that has a weak connection to the taxing jurisdiction and leads to multiple taxation. There is some merit to this argument, as discussed below, but economic issues do not tell the whole story.

A few high profile controversies (e.g., *Barclays Bank*) involving European governments and European businesses and the United States' state formulary apportionment method may have prejudiced EU governments and businesses against the method. By the time the Ruding Committee issued its report in 1992, formulary apportionment (or unitary taxation, as it is also known) had acquired a bad reputation in Europe.

This reputation developed in several areas over an extended period of time. The controversy began at the U.S. state level in the early 1970s in a case concerning the state of California and Shell Petroleum, NV, a European multinational enterprise.[19] The issue became a Federal and international irritant in the late 1970s when controversy erupted over a provision in the U.S.-U.K. income tax treaty that would have limited the U.S. states' ability to apply combined reporting with formulary apportionment on a worldwide basis.[20]

The controversy continued into the 1980s when the U.S. Supreme Court upheld state application of worldwide combined reporting for domestic-based companies.[21] Although the case involved a U.S. company, European governments became concerned that worldwide combined reporting would spread to other states, thereby bringing additional income into the tax bases of U.S. states.

Pressures from the U.S. Federal government (and, indirectly, from European and other governments) encouraged the states to eliminate mandatory worldwide combined reporting by the mid-1980s.[22] These state legislative changes, however, did not fully resolve European concerns.

By the early 1990s, the Europeans were engaged in a battle at the U.S. Supreme Court in the *Barclays Bank* case involving the state of California's use of worldwide combined reporting. This time, however, the company involved was a European-based company.[23] When the U.S. Supreme Court again ruled in favor of the state, many European companies and governments were convinced that worldwide combined reporting with formulary apportionment was a tax nightmare.

Although the state tax issue involves the question of the extent of a U.S. state's tax jurisdiction, rather than the relative merits of formulary versus arm's length apportionment, the cumulative impact of these controversies was an unyielding opposition by European governments to any type of tax method that invoked a formula.[24]

This opposition reached its peak during the process of updating the OECD transfer pricing guidelines. As Durst and Culbertson (2003) explain, the allegation that a transfer pricing method "invoked a formulary method was considered in itself by some to be a sufficient criticism of the merits of the method."[25] The innovative profit-based approaches to transfer pricing under discussion in the United States never had a chance of being accepted internationally once they had been accused of having formulary characteristics.[26]

In evaluating potential updates to the OECD transfer pricing guidelines, foreign governments appeared to link the new U.S. profit-based transfer pricing methods designed to be applied within an arm's length system with the controversy over California's application of worldwide combined reporting and formulary apportionment. They appeared to view both issues as unwarranted attempts to increase U.S. taxable income at the expense of foreign governments or as an example of unrelieved double taxation.

Opposition to formulary apportionment of worldwide profits at the U.S. state level, thus, extended into opposition to all formulary methods, or methods perceived as similar to formulary methods, at the international level. This blanket opposition likely prevented any rational discussion of the benefits of formulary apportionment within the European Union.

These two decades of controversy, perhaps more than any other reason, explain the general European opposition to formulary methods of any type, even though that opposition should rationally apply only to certain applications of formulary apportionment and combined reporting.

1.5 INTRODUCING FORMULARY APPORTIONMENT INTO THE SINGLE MARKET

Given this deep-seated aversion to formulary-based methods in the European Union, how was it possible for the European Commission to present a company tax reform for the European Union that moves away from the arm's length principle and toward formulary apportionment? Why does the EU business community now generally support a company tax system that incorporates formulary apportionment in the European Union?

The answers lie in several areas. By the time the European Commission released its Study in 2001, the European Union had undergone significant economic changes. In the early 1990s, the European Community was just setting out on its goal to create a unified EU market. By 2001, the Member States had eliminated many of the non-tax barriers to cross-border activity in the European Union. As a result, many EU companies had organized their EU operations at the EU level.

At the dawn of the Single Market in 1992, many academics examined the types of company tax systems that might be appropriate for taxing multinational enterprises in the Single Market and found formulary apportionment a practical and feasible response to the business developments in the Single Market.[27] It took another decade for the European Commission to come to this view.

By 2001, the vehement opposition to formulary apportionment and arguably similar methods that characterized much of the 1990s had significantly softened. As the European economy became more and more integrated, EU businesses and European tax authorities slowly shifted their views of the arm's length transfer pricing process toward a greater acceptance of profit-based methods.

For example, although the OECD Transfer Pricing Guidelines reject global formulary apportionment, the Guidelines do adopt new profit-based transfer pricing methods.[28] Although not all EU governments support the new methods to the same degree, by approving the OECD Guidelines with the profit-split methods, the international community validated the use of these profit-based methods. Thus, the dichotomy between formulary methods and arm's length methods has significantly narrowed and, in many cases, almost disappeared.

In addition the U.S. states had successfully resolved the international conflict over the use of global formulary apportionment by implementing legislation that allowed (or required) multinational companies to limit the scope of the apportionment system to the United States.[29] Once the states had scaled back the geographical scope of their tax systems, formulary apportionment no longer created the perceived risk of double taxation and excessive compliance burdens that had arisen when some U.S. states made its global application mandatory.

Most importantly, perhaps, the growing difficulties that EU multinational enterprises face in applying the separate accounting with arm's length pricing method coupled with increased enforcement by the tax authorities has also helped EU multinationals see formulary apportionment in a different light. Accompanying these changes is the view that the European Union should apply a company tax system that is better suited than the current method for taxing companies in an integrated market.[30] The approach of treating each integrated enterprise as a collection of unrelated and independent entities may have appeared appropriate when these enterprises mostly did business within a single Member State and had few cross-border transactions to price. The method also was relatively easy to implement when companies engaged in simple cross-border transactions involving the transfer of tangible goods that had readily identifiable comparable market prices.

The 21st century picture is a very different one in the European Union. The cross-border integration of EU multinational enterprises has sharply increased the volume and altered the nature of cross-border transactions. Cross-border transactions now frequently involve unique, difficult-to-price intangibles within highly integrated enterprises, making it difficult, if not impossible to find comparable transactions required to meet the arm's length principle. Treating the related members of an EU multinational enterprise as independent entities transferring tangible goods no longer reflects typical business operations. The creation of pan-European operations by many EU multinational enterprises has largely made national EU Member State borders irrelevant --- except for Member State tax purposes.

From a tax administration point of view, although it may not guarantee a "correct" profit allocation in the traditional sense, formulary apportionment appears better suited to avoid double taxation problems in the EU than the arm's length transfer pricing system. The scope for disagreement about the elements of the formulary approach seems narrower than the scope for disagreement about the arm's length transfer prices. Member State tax bases may be less vulnerable to inappropriate income shifting under formulary apportionment than under separate accounting.

As the OECD (2003a) notes, the economic integration in the EU has caused the European Commission and many Member States to "rethink their stand against formulary apportionment within the EU." The almost knee-jerk rejection of formulary apportionment seems, in hindsight, to have been an over-reaction based on opposition to the use of formulary apportionment on a worldwide unitary basis in a handful of U.S. states. This opposition may have perpetuated the existence of company tax obstacles in the European Union longer than necessary.

In an attempt to redress what he views as an imbalance in the frequency and harshness of criticisms directed at one of the two analytical approaches to transfer pricing, Rosenbloom (2005) notes, "it is not only the formulary approach that has flaws in theory, concept and method." Rosenbloom suggests that if constructed properly and in the right context, a formulary approach might eliminate many current controversies over the arm's length process.

It is not realistic to expect the politically-independent countries around the world to reach sufficient agreement on the elements of an apportionment system to make it feasible as the basic international method for taxing multinational enterprises. However, it does seem realistic that in the EU context, the Member States can construct a proper formulary apportionment approach for taxing companies within a Single Market.

The next chapter discusses the landscape for company tax reform in the European Union and how formulary apportionment fits into that landscape.

Notes

1. See Commission of the European Communities Communication "Towards an Internal Market without tax obstacles. A strategy for providing companies with a consolidated corporate tax base for their EU-wide activities" [COM(2001)582] and Study "Company Taxation in the

Internal Market" [SEC(2001)1681]. The Commission released both documents on October 23, 2001 and later released the Study as a book in 2002. All references to the Study are to the 2002 book. See Commission (2001, 2002). The system would be optional for Member States and for multinational enterprises. For a description of the Study, see Weiner (2001b). For analyses of the proposals, see Westberg (2002) and Mintz (2002).

2. The use of the term "formulary apportionment" in this context includes applying formulary apportionment on a combined or consolidated group basis. Consolidated or combined reporting ignores the separate legal entity structure (once common ownership exceeds a certain threshold) and combines the income of a group of affiliated corporations into a single measure of income. Internal transactions are eliminated in calculating consolidated income; thus the transfer pricing problem is largely removed. Formulary apportionment involves allocating total income across locations using a pre-determined formula. Although the Canadian provinces and some U.S. states apply formulary apportionment on a separate entity basis, as a practical matter at the international level, since multinational enterprises generally operate in foreign countries through subsidiaries, formulary apportionment would apply on a consolidated basis. It is for this reason that applying formulary apportionment to a consolidated tax base is a comprehensive EU company tax reform. See Wetzler (1995) for a concise explanation of this point.

3. A "transfer price" is the price an enterprise sets for the internal transfers within the divisions of the enterprise. When an enterprise does business in more than one country, it may set transfer prices to value the operations in each country. The transfer price, thus, is an important element in determining the taxable income associated with each entity and, therefore, with each country. For tax purposes, these transfer prices must be set according to the arm's length principle, as discussed later.

4. As Jerome Hellerstein (1982) remarked, "The Achilles heel of separate accounting is the inability to establish fair arm's length prices for goods transferred, or basic operational services rendered, between controlled branches or subsidiaries of an enterprise." As Walter Hellerstein (2005) recently explained, "A key reason to employ formulary apportionment, whether to a single corporation or to a group of commonly controlled corporations, is because they are engaged in integrated cross-border economic activity that cannot readily be treated on an arm's length/ separate-geographic accounting basis."

5. Spain used "fractional apportionment" until the mid-20th century to tax foreign enterprises. See Raventós-Calvo and de Juan y Peñalosa (2002) for details of the Spanish history. Germany uses formulary methods for the local trade tax.

6. EU business representatives emphasize that they condition their support for any comprehensive solution on the new rules being optional, that is, that companies may decide to remain taxed under the individual Member State tax systems. See UNICE (2000, 2004). Not all UNICE members support the Commission's strategy.

7. The U.S. states and the Canadian provinces initially preferred to use separate accounting, but over time, separate accounting disappeared in favor of formulary apportionment. In the Canadian provinces, Smith (1976) reports that "The separate accounts rule was dropped because so few companies were using it and it was an administrative headache. Besides, it detracted from the uniformity of the general rule." At that time, a company had the option of calculating its income in the province on the basis of the permanent establishment's separate accounts (computed as if it operated as an independent enterprise), or to use a formula if the separate accounts were not available. At roughly the same time, the U.S. states were developing a set of uniform rules that provided for formulary apportionment and allowed for separate accounting only on request or if required by the tax authority. By the 1950s, the U.S. states had also generally moved to formulary apportionment due largely because of business preference for the method over separate accounting. For further discussion of Canadian history, see Smith (1998), and Bird and Brean (1986). For U.S. history, see Hellerstein and Hellerstein (1998, cum Supp. 2005) and Weiner (1999).

8. The European Commission (2004a) makes it clear that it endorses a common consolidated corporate tax base on an EU-wide basis, but it has not provided details on the contours of this system. Given the lack of details over the potential proposal, including the exact form that the tax base and apportionment mechanism may take, the analysis in this text focuses on issues involved in applying formulary apportionment to a consolidated EU-level tax base in the European Union.

9. This choice is practical. Much of the history and empirical analysis draws from the author's dissertation, which evaluated the experiences in the U.S. states and Canadian provinces in relation to implementing formulary apportionment in the European Community. See Weiner (1994). For a recent analysis of these issues conducted for the European Commission, see Weiner (2005).

10. For additional details, see the OECD (1995) report *Transfer Pricing Guidelines for Multinational Enterprises and Tax Administrations.*

11. Participants also thought it would be difficult for countries to agree on a common apportionment formula. Langbein (1986) credits the Carroll Report (1933) and the work of the Fiscal Committee of the League of Nations in drafting the first model income tax convention in 1935 as giving birth to the arm's length method as an international standard. For analyses of the development of the separate accounting with arm's length pricing method and its adoption as the international standard, see Avi-Yonah (1995), Graetz and O'Hear (1997), and Langbein (1986).

At the same time that the international community was considering how to design a system for taxing multinational corporations, the U.S. states were considering how to design a system for taxing multistate corporations. As part of this process, the states examined whether the same principles that were applicable at the international level also held at the state level. They came to the conclusion that the methods appropriate in the international sphere could not always be applied to the allocation of income on an interstate basis. The states preferred apportionment to separate entity accounting because it had proved to be an easy and simple method of assigning income to the various taxing states. See Gerstenberg (1931).

12. The United States refers to the arm's length standard, while the OECD refers to the arm's length principle.

13. For an evaluation of issues that arise with using separate-entity accounting as an allocation method under U.S. rules, see Shay, Fleming, and Peroni (2002). See McDaniel and Ault (1998) for a description of the international tax rules in the United States.

14. See Gresik (2001) for a discussion of the tracing and allocation approaches followed in selected countries. Some countries follow a tracing approach where they attempt to match expenses with the income while other countries follow an allocation approach where they apply a formula to allocate expenses between domestic and foreign sources. Countries that exempt foreign-source income, such as the Netherlands, tend to apply the tracing approach while countries that tax worldwide income, such as the United States, tend to apply the allocation approach. See also McDaniel (1994) for a discussion of areas in which the United States applies formulary methods for federal purposes.

15. See the Report by the European Round Table (ERT) and the Union of Industrial and Employers' Confederations of Europe (UNICE) (1999). As mentioned above, transfer prices set for business purposes may not necessarily be the ones set for tax purposes.

16. The Commission reviews these efforts in its Study (2002).

17. For the Ruding Report and the Commission's response, see Commission (1992a, b). For an evaluation of the Ruding Report by a Committee member, see Vanistendael (1992).

18. As Albert Rädler, a member of the Ruding Committee, recalled, "formulary apportionment was a 'devil's word'" when writing the Ruding Report. Dr. Rädler made this comment during an electronic forum where participants debated the then recently released Commission Study. For a transcript of that debate, see Tax Analysts (2002). As discussed below in a legal case involving U.S. state worldwide combined reporting with formulary apportionment and Shell

Petroleum, a Dutch company, Onno Ruding, who was the Netherlands' Finance Minister at that time, sent a letter to the U.S. Treasury Department in September 1983 requesting that Treasury support any initiatives that would end the states' use of worldwide combined reporting. Thus, it is understandable that it may have been difficult for the Ruding Committee to support formulary apportionment for the European Union. In recalling this history, the OECD (2003a) reports that much of the developed world opposed worldwide combined reporting by some American states, and "in 1992, the Ruding Committee summarily dismissed global formulary apportionment."

19. The case concerned the fact that California included in the state tax base the parent company's European profits, which had the effect of not only offsetting the losses its California subsidiary incurred but also of making that subsidiary profitable for state tax purposes. The company contended that the businesses were unrelated and the state could not combine the foreign income in the state tax base. See *Shell Petroleum NV v. Graves* 570 F. Supp 58 (N.D. Cal.), aff'd 709 F. 2d 593 (9th Cir.), cert denied, 464 S. Ct. 1012 (1983). The U.S. Supreme Court declined to hear the case due to issues relating to the "standing" of the foreign parent company.

Shell Petroleum, NV, was a Netherlands holding company jointly owned by the Royal Dutch Petroleum Co. and the Shell Transport and Trading Company. Among its holdings were Shell Oil Company and Scallop Nuclear, Inc. that did business in California. Upon audit, the California Franchise Tax Board determined that the Scallop Company was engaged in a unitary business with Shell Petroleum and thus required to file on a worldwide combined reporting basis. As a result, the Scallop Nuclear corporation had taxable state income of $46 million (a figure that the tax authorities later revised) rather than the $390 million in losses the company reported from 1973 to 1976.

California began regularly applying the unitary combined report on a worldwide basis in the late 1960s. Miller (1984) reports that the first "decision of record" in California involving foreign-parent combination involved tax payments from 1968-1970 by Beecham, Inc., which was a subsidiary of the Beecham Group, a United Kingdom company. In 1977, the California Board of Equalization ruled that Beecham was unitary with its U.S. operations and, thus, liable for the state tax as determined under formulary apportionment. The Board of Equalization reasoned "strictly as a logical proposition, that foreign source income is no different from any other income when it comes to determining, by formulary apportionment, the appropriate share of the income of a unitary business taxable by a particular state." See *Appeal of Beecham, Inc., Cal. St. Bd. Of Equalization*, March 2, 1977. See Miller (1984) for the history of worldwide combined reporting in California.

20. Worldwide combined reporting with formulary apportionment took center stage in 1976 when, after years of negotiations, the United States and the United Kingdom released the text of a newly-signed bilateral income tax treaty. As with all treaties, the negotiators attempted to reach a balance among perceived compromises, although there is no direct quid pro quo among provisions. On the U.S. side, the U.S. agreed to a provision, Article 9(4), which would limit the states' ability to use worldwide combined reporting. On the U.K. side, the U.K. agreed to grant partial relief to U.S. investors for the U.K. advance corporation tax (ACT).

U.K. objections to the states' use of worldwide combined reporting are well known. However, the U.S. objections to the U.K. ACT refund are less-well documented but equally important to understand the controversy.

The United Kingdom had introduced a partially integrated system in 1973 that denied the integration credit to foreign shareholders. Since the European Commission had introduced a draft proposal in 1975 calling for a similar integration system in all Member States of the European Community, the United States was concerned that this partial integration system might spread throughout the European Community to the disadvantage of U.S. shareholders.

In the United States, treaties are negotiated by the Executive Branch of government but then must be approved by a two-thirds vote of the Senate on behalf of the Legislative Branch. The U.S. Senate did not accept the use of a tax treaty to restrict state sovereignty, even though the treaty provided a clear benefit to U.S. investors in the form of the ACT refund. The U.S.-U.K. Tax Treaty failed to achieve the two-thirds approval required for ratification.

The controversy over the treaty lasted nearly four years as the U.S. Congress attempted to balance the interests of those in favor of protecting states' rights with the interests of those who desired to obtain the benefits from the ACT refund. Since only a few states applied the worldwide combined reporting method, the issue was not of great concern to most states; by contrast, a large number of companies would benefit from the ACT refund. The two countries finally brought the treaty into force when the U.K. approved the revised treaty that no longer contained the provision restricting U.S. state tax practices. The final treaty did, however, continue to grant the partial ACT refund to U.S. shareholders. See United States-United Kingdom Income Tax Convention, Dec. 31, 1975, as amended by an Exchange of Notes, signed on April 13, 1976, and Protocols, signed on Aug. 26, 1976, March 31, 1977, and March 15, 1979, eff. April 25, 1980. For analysis, see Schoettle (1977), Kline (1983), and Devgun (1996).

21. See *Container Corp. v. Franchise Tax Board*, 463 U.S. 159 (1983). This case was one of five cases the Supreme Court considered from 1980 to 1983 addressing the validity of various aspects of unitary combined reporting.

The Court acknowledged the difficulties it faced, reasoning that "[A]llocating income among various taxing jurisdictions bears some resemblance . . . to slicing a shadow." Both geographical accounting and formulary apportionment are "imperfect proxies for an ideal" that is difficult to achieve in practice and in theory. In this ruling, the Supreme Court noted that in addition to "control" there must be a "flow of value" among affiliated corporations for the business to be unitary.

An interesting point for the EU Member States to consider in the context of restricting formulary apportionment to the EU's territorial borders is that the application of combined reporting and formulary apportionment within the United States was not at issue. Moreover, the dissent in the 5 to 3 decision reasoned that California could avoid the international implications by basing its apportionment calculations on the taxpayer's U.S. income as reported on its federal tax return. This amount is calculated by the arm's length method and is therefore consistent with international practice.

22. The U.S. Congress considered legislation that would restrict state use of worldwide unitary combination. See, for example, the bill drafted by the Reagan Administration and introduced into the Congress in December 1985 as S. 1974 ("The Unitary Tax Repealer Act") and H.R. 3980, 99th Cong., 1st Sess. 1985. Despite repeated attempts, the Congress has never enacted any such legislation.

23. In 1994, the Supreme Court upheld the application of the California tax method to a foreign-based parent. See *Barclays Bank PLC v. Franchise Tax Board*, 512 U.S., 129 L.Ed.2d 244 (1994). The Barclays Bank case concerned tax payments in the 1970s, which was before California made the water's edge election available.

California was not the only state under examination. Reuters Limited, a subsidiary of Reuters Holdings PLC, a United Kingdom company, was then a party to litigation with the New York State tax authorities challenging the constitutionality of New York State's worldwide reporting requirements.

As far back as 1918 a formulary approach had been applied to a British company and been approved by the United States Supreme Court. See *Bass, Ratcliff & Gretton Ltd. v. State Tax Commission* 266 US 271 (1924).

European governments made their opposition to worldwide combined reporting loud and clear when the Barclays Bank litigation was active. The U.S. Supreme Court noted that a "battalion of foreign governments" had "marched to Barclays' aid'", deploring worldwide combined reporting in diplomatic notes, amicus briefs, and even retaliatory legislation." (For a discussion of issues involved in the Barclays Bank controversy, see the U.S. Supreme Court's decision and accompanying briefs.)

The Court noted that the governments of many of the U.S.' trading partners had expressed their strong disapproval of California's method of taxation, as demonstrated by the amici briefs in support of Barclays from the Government of the United Kingdom, and from the Member States of the European Communities (Belgium, Denmark, France, Germany, Greece, Ireland, Italy, Luxembourg, the Netherlands, Portugal, Spain and the United Kingdom) and the Governments of Australia, Austria, Canada, Finland, Japan, Norway, Sweden, and Switzerland. The Court also noted that Barclays drew its attention to the fact that the U.S. State Department reported that it "has received diplomatic notes complaining about state use of the worldwide unitary method of taxation from virtually every developed country in the world." (See footnote 22 in Barclays.) These countries condemned the method as being "contradictory to, and incompatible with, accepted international principles of corporate tax assessment and the purpose of double taxation and/or friendship, commerce and navigation treaties to which the United States is a party; and is an impediment to investment and trade with the U.S."

The British Parliament had enacted, but not implemented, retaliatory legislation. The particular legislation, which was adopted unanimously on July 9, 1985, was known as the Grylls clause after Sir Michael Grylls, a back bench conservative member of Parliament. See Finance Act, 1985, ch. 54, Sec 54 & sch. 13 reenacted as Income and Corporation Taxes Act, 1988, ch. 1, sections 812-815 (United Kingdom). The legislation, which would have denied the ACT refunds, would have over-ridden the provisions of Article 10(2) of the U.S.-U.K. income tax treaty in breach of the U.K.'s treaty obligations. In 1993, the British Government again threatened retaliation against U.S. corporations with U.K. subsidiaries if the states had not satisfactorily solved the problem by the end of the year. See Coffill (1993) for a discussion of the compromises California made in the water's edge reporting system in 1993 to respond to the divergent interests of foreign-based and California-based multinationals.

24. Other countries, including Japan and Canada, also strongly opposed the worldwide combined reporting method. Canada's opposition is interesting since Canada employs formulary apportionment, but only within the provinces. For a discussion of the Canadian view, see Brown (1984). See also the case involving Alcan Aluminum and the state of Oregon (*Alcan Aluminum Ltd. V. Dept. of Revenue*, 724F. 2d 1294 (7th Cir. 1984). Alcan Aluminum also had active litigation in California. See *Alcan Aluminum Ltd. v. Franchise Tax Board*, 558 F. Supp. 624 (SDNY 1983).

25. See the U.S. Department of the Treasury (1988) *Study of Intercompany Pricing Under Section 482 of the Code* (The White Paper) for a discussion of the new "basic arm's length rate of return method (BALRM)." The criticisms mounted as Treasury transformed the methods proposed in the White Paper into proposed transfer pricing regulations in 1992. See Avi-Yonah (1995) for a summary of the official comments.

26. See the letter from the Secretary General of UNICE to the U.S. Treasury Department expressing the concern of many European investors with the alleged deviation from the arm's length principle in the 1993 revised proposed and temporary transfer pricing regulations. See UNICE (1994). The fact that the Barclays Bank case was active while the OECD was updating its Transfer Pricing Guidelines did not help make formulary-based transfer pricing methods acceptable at the OECD.

27. See McLure (1989), Goldsworth (1989), Weiner (1992), Munnell (1992), Summers (1988), and Musgrave (1972), among others.

28. See Culbertson (1990) for an analysis of the similarities between the profit-based methods in the U.S. regulations and in the OECD Guidelines. The OECD's profit methods include a profit-split method and a transactional net margin method that is conceptually similar to an explicit profit split method. The OECD approved profit-based methods apply a formula that is specific to each firm while the rejected global formulary apportionment method applies a pre-determined formula to all firms.

29. See Ferguson (1986) for a discussion of state legislative actions to move away from world-wide combined reporting and McLure and Weiner (2000) for a list of the states and the legislative actions taken.

30. For a discussion of this issue in the U.S. state context, see the Willis Committee of the U.S. Congress (1964), as reprinted in Weiner (1999). The Committee found that separate accounting was not a feasible method for the states, noting that ". . . [The arm's length approach] . . . would be virtually impossible to administer at the State level as applied to interstate transactions. Thus, there is no significant disagreement that the states must use some type of apportionment formula (as distinguished from making an allocation of income and deductions by separate accounting), since there would be no practical way of determining what income of a company is earned within a state as opposed to being earned within other states (or in foreign countries)."

Chapter 2

THE LANDSCAPE FOR EU COMPANY TAX REFORM

Through the Treaty of Rome, six European countries founded the European Economic Community fifty years ago and committed to "lay the foundations of an ever closer union among the peoples of Europe."[1] In the half century since then, the European Economic Community has undergone profound changes in how it operates as it has grown to a membership of twenty-five countries and become the European Union. Yet, the over-riding economic goals remain the same: To adopt policies and laws that will help create a common market; to abolish obstacles to the free movement of goods, services, labor and capital; and to provide for freedom of establishment.

2.1 FOREIGN DIRECT INVESTMENT AND TAXATION

The European Union's economic structure has evolved since the mid-20th century. Currency exchange controls no longer exist among Member States. Twelve Member States use a single currency. The Member States are adopting common international financial reporting standards and they are eliminating withholding taxes on cross-border intra-company dividend, interest, and royalty payments. They have established procedures to create a "European Company" and are removing the tax disadvantages to cross-border mergers in the EU.

The reduction in internal barriers in the Single Market may be a factor in the growth in foreign investment into the European Union. Since the European Community launched the Single Market initiative in 1992, foreign direct investment in the EU has grown more than twice as fast as EU income. Foreign direct investment flows in and out of the EU reached record levels at the end of the 20th century.[2] The number of cross-border mergers and acquisitions within the EU rose by 55 percent during the 1990s; intra-EU mergers and acquisitions amounted to roughly 70 percent of the total during the 1990s.[3]

In addition to the reduction in non-tax barriers, the overall reduction in corporate income tax rates in the European Union may also help explain these increased flows. The average tax rate in the EU-15 Member States is nearly ten percentage points lower now than it was a decade ago. A second factor is the downward pressure on company tax rates as the European Union accepts new members. Apart from Malta and the Czech Republic, the tax rates in the new Member States are generally well below the rates in the EU-15 (except for in Ireland). Table 1 shows this downward trend in tax rates for the EU-15 and the ten new Member States for selected years.

The growth in cross-border investment flows has made EU businesses highly aware of the additional costs they incur when they do business in another Member State. The fact that compliance burdens increase when EU companies expand across border should come as no surprise. Each EU Member State largely operates its company tax system as if it were an autonomous system with few links to other EU Member States.[4]

The Commission Study (2002) finds that the variation in Member State tax bases is so great that it is not possible to identify a common approach among ten central tax base elements. Some Member States offer accelerated depreciation, while others offer straight-line depreciation. Some value inventory on a first-in, first-out basis; others follow the last-in, first-out rule. Subject to Commission approval under state aid provisions, all offer investment tax credits and tax incentives for specific forms of investment. Depreciation rates vary across Member States with the type of asset, such as industrial buildings, intangible property, plant, machinery, and office equipment. Finkenzeller and Spengel (2004) show that the addition of ten new Member States has reduced the average level of corporate tax rates, but has not reduced the variation in company tax systems.

The Commission identifies the existence of twenty-five separate tax systems in the EU as the underlying cause of these additional compliance burdens. As the Commission Study (2002) notes, "The need to comply with a multiplicity of different rules entails a considerable compliance cost and represents in itself a significant barrier to cross-border economic activity" in the European Union.

To describe the tax situation in the enlarged European Union as a "tax jungle" is not far off the mark. Nor, in the midst of this tax jungle is it surprising that EU multinational enterprises seek a path toward a "better" tax system.

2.2   CROSS-BORDER TAX ISSUES IN THE EUROPEAN UNION

Cross-border loss compensation

In terms of specific obstacles to cross-border investment in the European Union, the Commission Study (2002) reports "the absence of cross-border loss

Table 1. Corporate income tax rates in the EU-15 and in the new EU Member States, selected years

EU-15 Member State	1995	2000	2004	2005
Austria	34%	34%	34%	25%
Belgium	40.2	40.2	34	34
Denmark	34	32	30	30
Finland	25	29	29	26
France	36.7	36.7	35.4	35.4
Germany	56.8	51.6	38.3	38.3
Greece	40	40	35	35
Ireland	40	24	12.5	12.5
Italy	52.2	41.3	37.3	37.3
Luxembourg	35	35	30.4	30.4
Netherlands	35	35	34.5	34.5
Portugal	39.6	35.2	27.5	27.5
Spain	35	35	35	35
Sweden	28	28	28	28
United Kingdom	33	30	30	30
New Member State	**1995**	**2000**	**2004**	**2005**
Czech Republic	41%	31%	28%	26%
Cyprus	25	29	15	10
Estonia	26	26	26	26
Hungary	19.6	19.6	17.7	16
Latvia	25	25	15	15
Lithuania	25	25	15	15
Malta	35	35	35	35
Poland	40	30	19	19
Slovakia	40	29	19	19
Slovenia	25	25	25	25
Average EU-15	38.0%	35.3%	31.4%	30.6%
Average new EU-10	30.6	27.4	21.5	20.6

Note: As of 2000 and until 2008, Estonia taxes distributed earnings at 26 percent but exempts retained earnings from tax. Source: Table II-5.1 in Structures of the taxation systems in the European Union, Eurostat (2004).

relief or full consolidation at the EU level as one of the major obstacles that re-quires action as a matter of priority." Table 2 shows that although all but a half-dozen Member States offer domestic loss offsetting, only a handful of Member States (Austria, Denmark, and Italy) generally allow companies to offset losses of foreign subsidiaries against domestic profits.[5]

The lack of cross-border compensation for losses of foreign subsidiaries has several potential consequences. It may affect whether a company organizes its foreign operations as branches or as subsidiaries; it may also affect whether a company decides to undertake foreign investment at all.

Table 2. Domestic and cross-border loss offsetting in the EU Member States, 2005

| | Domestic Loss Offsetting | | Group Taxation | |
	Carry Back	Carry Forward	Domestic	Cross Border
Austria	none	unlimited	loss transfer	yes
Belgium	none	unlimited	no	no
Cyprus	none	unlimited	loss transfer	no
Czech Rep.	none	5 years	no	no
Denmark	none	unlimited	pooling	yes
Estonia	n.a.	n.a.	n.a.	no
Finland	none	10 years	loss transfer	no
France	3 year option	unlimited	pooling	limited
Germany	1 year option	unlimited	pooling	no
Greece	none	unlimited	no	no
Hungary	none	unlimited	no	no
Ireland	1 year option	unlimited	loss transfer	no
Italy	none	5 years	pooling	yes
Latvia	none	5 years	loss transfer	no
Lithuania	none	5 years	no	no
Luxembourg	none	unlimited	pooling	no
Malta	none	unlimited	loss transfer	no
Netherlands	3 year required	unlimited	tax consolid.	no
Poland	none	5 years	pooling	no
Portugal	none	6 years	pooling	no
Slovakia	none	5 years	no	no
Slovenia	none	5 years	pooling	no
Spain	none	15 years	pooling	no
Sweden	none	unlimited	loss transfer	no
U.K.	1 year option	unlimited	loss transfer	no

Notes: n.a. means 'not available." Source: Commission (2005b).

Providing cross-border loss compensation, however, does not address a fundamental issue facing EU multinational enterprises. Even if each Member State offered cross-border loss offsetting, each entity would still calculate its own tax base. Enterprises would be able to offset losses, but they would not have a single consolidated tax base and they would still face the transfer pricing obstacle, as discussed below. No Member State offers what the European Commission and EU businesses have endorsed: cross-border consolidation of EU-level profits.

Transfer pricing documentation requirements

In addition to the difficulties they face establishing arm's length transfer prices, the EU businesses report another concern about the transfer pricing process: The growing documentation burden.

If a taxpayer fails to follow the arm's length principle when setting transfer prices, the tax authority may reallocate income to obtain an arm's length result.[6] To avoid such a re-allocation, the taxpayer must prove that it established its transfer prices on an arm's length basis. Part of this proof is demonstrated through supplying documentary evidence.

As a result, complying with the arm's length principle can become a burdensome process.[7] The OECD (2004b) shows that all of the EU members in the OECD now require companies to maintain written records. The European Commission (2004d) survey of compliance costs showed that more than 80 percent of the additional compliance costs that arise when conducting cross-border business relate to transfer pricing documentation requirements.

To some extent, these greater transfer pricing enforcement efforts are a new development for many EU governments. As Durst and Culbertson (2003) suggest, countries outside of the United States in the past generally were "content with the historical levels of enforcement (or, as often seems to have been the case, non-enforcement) generally found around the world."[8]

That situation has changed. EU and non-EU companies surveyed by Ernst & Young (1997, 1999, 2001, 2003) report that tax authorities are increasing their focus on transfer pricing enforcement. In its 1999 Report, for example, Ernst & Young report a "hardening attitude on tax-driven transfer pricing" among 19 EU and non-EU countries surveyed. The 1999 report continues that "[t]he strict U.S.-initiated transfer pricing model (with accompanying documentation requirements, penalties, and enforcement) is spreading quickly to other nations around the globe and adding to the strain."

The Ernst & Young 2003 Global Survey reports that multinational companies view audits by tax authorities as the rule, rather than an exception. For example, 9 out of 10 Danish respondents, 8 out of 10 German respondents, and 7 out of 10 Finnish respondents indicate that tax revenue authorities are paying close attention to transfer pricing issues, thus triggering additional transfer pricing disputes.

The European Commission (2003b) identifies certain incompatibilities with the transfer pricing process and the Internal Market. As reported in its Internal Market Scoreboard, although EU multinational companies have arrangements to solve the transfer pricing problem, "the whole process of computing the correct price, preparing the supporting documentation and finding agreements to resolve disputes is costly and time consuming for both business and administrations."

In light of the increased emphasis on the proper application of the arm's length principle, the criticism by EU businesses that complying with the transfer pricing rules may create an unreasonable compliance burden is understandable. If EU tax authorities had generally taken a "relaxed view" towards transfer pricing practices until the 1990s, then the fact that the transfer pricing rules "required" companies to apply the arm's length principle did not create a significant compliance burden.[9] If EU tax authorities have strengthened their enforcement of the arm's length principle and are penalizing taxpayers for failing to provide sufficient documentary proof, then EU businesses may be open to alternative, less burdensome methods of allocating their tax bases across the Member States.

The view from EU governments

EU governments face challenging issues enforcing the separate accounting with arm's length pricing principle. The European Commission (2004a) explains that EU Member State tax systems are increasingly vulnerable to "tax evasion and fraud which exploits precisely the weaknesses of separate accounting . . . Moreover, the current system is costing both companies and tax authorities dearly in terms of administrative and compliance costs." As shown earlier, as the barriers to cross-border investment have fallen, EU multinationals have expanded their operations throughout the European Union. This increased cross-border expansion creates additional concerns for tax authorities that their tax bases may become increasingly vulnerable to erosion.

This concern is particularly great in the Member States with relatively high tax rates. As long as tax rates differ across Member States, multinational enterprises have an incentive to locate their income in low-tax Member States and their expenses in high-tax Member States. For example, every 100 euros of profits taxed at 20 percent instead of at 45 percent potentially saves the MNE 25 euros. Ignoring the potentially offsetting effects relating to how the home country treats the foreign income of its resident companies, the benefit to income shifting equals the difference in tax rates, and the greater the difference in rates, the greater the incentive to shift income.[10]

Income shifting can occur in many ways. For example, an MNE may shift income to its low-tax subsidiary by charging it a low price for internal transfers of goods, or it may shift expenses into its high-tax subsidiary by charging above market interest rates on internal loans. If transfer prices are not subject to market forces, then the resulting income distribution may not reflect each entity's "true" income.[11]

Table 3 provides a simple illustration of how an integrated multinational enterprise may adjust the internal transfer price to shift income from a high tax to a low tax area. In this example, an Irish manufacturing company distributes its product through a British distributor. For simplicity, assume the Irish tax rate is 10 percent and the British tax rate is 30 percent.

In scenario (1), the British distributor is independent and in scenario (2) the British distributor is a controlled subsidiary of the Irish manufacturing company. With the relatively high tax rate in the UK, the newly-integrated multinational enterprise has the incentive to shift income from the UK to Ireland to reduce its total tax payments and, therefore, increase its total after-tax profits.

As discussed earlier, if the UK subsidiary operated as an independent entity, then it would focus on maximizing its separate profits and scenario (1)

Table 3. Illustration of cross-border income shifting

(1) **No profit shifting.** Irish manufacturing company sells goods to independent distributors in the United Kingdom. (figures are in £000)

Irish manufacturing company		Independent British distributor	
Sales	£50,000	Sales	£100,000
Cost of materials	(10,000)		
Cost of manufacture	(20,000)	Cost of sales	(50,000)
Gross profit	20,000	Gross profit	50,000
		Distribution	(35,000)
Administration	(5,000)	Administration	(5,000)
Pre-tax profit	15,000	Pre-tax profit	10,000
Tax (10%)	(1,500)	Tax (30%)	(3,000)
	=====		=====
Profit after tax	13,500	Profit after tax	7,000

(2) **Profit shifting.** Irish manufacturing company increases the internal transfer price to its wholly-owned British distribution subsidiary

Irish manufacturing company		British distribution subsidiary	
Sales	£58,000	Sales	£100,000
Cost of materials	(10,000)		
Cost of manufacture	(20,000)	Cost of sales	(58,000)
Gross profit	28,000	Gross profit	42,000
		Distribution	(35,000)
Administration	(5,000)	Administration	(5,000)
Pre-tax profit	23,000	Pre-tax profit	2,000
Tax (10%)	(2,300)	Tax (30%)	(600)
	=====		=====
Profit after tax	20,700	Profit after tax	1,400

Summary	Scenario (1)	Scenario (2)
Total profit before tax	25,000	25,000
Total tax payments	4,500	2,900
Total profit after tax	20,500	22,100

Note: This example is modified from example INTM460160 in the U.K. Inland Revenue International Manual. See Inland Revenue (2005).

would continue to represent the "independent entity" outcome. However, if the subsidiary no longer operates as an independent entity, then its objective now forms part of the multinational's overall objective of maximizing the group's profits, rather than its separate entity profits. The outcome in scenario (2) no longer represents the outcome independent entities would have reached since the independent British distributor had £7,000 after-tax profits, but the controlled distributor has just £1,400 after-tax profits.

The UK government is concerned about the tax base reduction that occurs within the multinational company in scenario (2). In accordance with the arm's length principle, the UK government may re-adjust the company's accounts to reflect the result that independent parties would have reached. To avoid double taxation, the Irish competent authority then makes a corresponding (or, correlative) adjustment in the profits attributed to the Irish manufacturing company. The agreement among countries to apply the arm's length principle generally provides a basis for tax authorities to reach these agreements and, therefore, eliminate the double taxation that might otherwise arise. If the Irish competent authority, however, does not agree with the profit adjustment, the multinational enterprise may suffer double taxation.[12]

Evidence of income shifting

Table 3 provides evidence that income shifting may occur in theory. This section shows how income shifting occurs in practice.

The empirical evidence suggests that governments may not always be able to prevent improper income shifting. Using tax data for U.S. multinational companies, Newlon (2000) finds patterns of reported profitability and taxation that are consistent with income shifting. For example, foreign-controlled companies report lower taxable income as a share of assets or sales than their U.S.-controlled counterparts. Likewise, the reported profits of the foreign subsidiaries of U.S. multinationals are negatively related to the effective tax rate foreign operations face. Newlon cautions, however, that although the data may suggest income shifting, they also may mask important differences in the underlying companies and that a more rigorous statistical analysis is necessary to control for these differences.

Econometric studies that control for these underlying differences provide some evidence that multinational companies engage in profit shifting, although generally not to the extent suggested by the data described above. Grubert, Goodspeed, and Swenson (1993) and Grubert (1997), for example, examine the tax returns of U.S.-controlled and foreign-controlled U.S. companies and find that non-tax reasons, such as company age, industry, and exchange rates, explain a majority of the differences between the reported profits of these two groups of companies. The remaining differences in profitability may be due to income shifting or to other unobservable factors. Clausing (2003) presents evidence suggesting that corporate tax avoidance reduces government revenues from the corporate income tax. In a study using European data, Bartelsman and Beetsma (2003) find that revenues do not increase when countries raise their tax rates because reported profits fall. Altshuler and Goodspeed (2002) find that European countries engage in a tax rate competition. Grubert (2003) finds that subsidiaries of U.S. multinational companies located in high or low tax areas that have a strong incentive to shift income also have a significantly larger volume of intercompany transactions.

To summarize, the increased volume of cross-border investment in the European Union coupled with the greater transfer pricing enforcement efforts, has made EU businesses aware of the tax obstacle created by the transfer pricing process. From the tax authorities' view, multinational enterprises appear increasingly able to shift income inappropriately to low-tax areas, and the empirical evidence suggests that multinational enterprises do take advantage of cross-border tax differentials to shift income.

These economic forces are not the only forces pressuring Member States to adjust their company tax practices. Political and judicial forces are playing a growing role in shaping Member State company tax policy.

2.3   CREATING A SINGLE MARKET IN THE EUROPEAN UNION

The evolution in Europe from a number of independent countries to an integrated union of Member States helps explain the European Commission's motivation in proposing a comprehensive new direction in company taxation. The process of creating the Single European Market is not complete, yet the changes brought about by the elimination of barriers to cross-border investment have significantly affected how EU multinationals do business in the EU and how Member States tax EU multinationals.

The EU exerted its strongest efforts to create a Single Market thirty years after signing the Treaty of Rome when the then twelve Member States adopted the Single European Act (SEA). Through the SEA, the Member States established the goal of creating a Single Market without internal frontiers by the end of 1992. The Treaty on European Union, which came into force in 1993, further stimulated these efforts by creating a common economic and monetary policy.

Although it provided numerous measures to eliminate tax barriers to cross-border investment in the Internal Market, the SEA did not mandate company tax harmonization. Instead, it maintained the unanimity principle for company tax measures. The EU Member States have consistently rejected moves that would limit their ability to set company tax policy, regardless of any potential estimated benefits from company tax harmonization.[13]

The more recent "enhanced cooperation" procedure loosens the binding constraint imposed by the unanimity requirement in the company tax area. Under enhanced cooperation, a group of at least eight Member States may agree to take a policy forward, as long as this cooperation does not discriminate against non-participating Member States and does not undermine the economic cohesion of the internal market. Non-participating Member States may not impede implementation of the cooperative measures in the participating Member States.

The European Commission has the sole right to propose Community legislation, and it takes the leading role in proposing EU-level tax policy measures, but the Member States must approve these proposals. Apart from a few Directives and related measures, the Member States have rarely approved the Commission's company tax proposals.[14]

This rejection has many explanations, but it may primarily be due to the Member States' view that retaining complete autonomy to set company tax policy is paramount. Member States do not feel compelled to create an EU-level company tax system

Despite the unanimity principle and reluctance to undertake company tax reform at the EU level, the Member States have taken action in the general realm of company tax reform in one important area. Perhaps more than any other European Commission initiative, the Code of Conduct on Business Taxation that the EU Member States adopted as part of the Tax Package in 1997 is causing some convergence in company tax bases across the European Union. Through the Code of Conduct, Member States must eliminate their potentially harmful preferential tax practices. In also complying with state aid rules, Member States are eliminating many measures that cause company tax bases to diverge across Member States.

Despite these actions to eliminate specific harmful preferential tax regimes, however, the Member States have not yet focused on the importance of creating an EU-level company tax system. Each Member State continues to view its company tax objectives essentially in isolation from the objectives of the European Union as a whole.

2.4   INFLUENCES FROM THE EUROPEAN COURT OF JUSTICE

Recent actions from the European Court of Justice (ECJ), however, are forcing the Member States to take a broader look at how their company tax policies may be affecting the welfare of the European Union as a whole. The European Court of Justice is putting increasing pressure on the Member States to bring their company practices in line with their obligations under the EU Treaty.

Although the Member States may not yet agree, EU businesses feel that it is imperative to eliminate the measures in Member State company tax systems that hinder cross-border expansion in the European Union. The failure of the EU Member States to eliminate perceived discriminatory features of their company tax laws, combined with the inability of the European Commission to push through EU company tax reforms, has forced EU companies to turn to

Table 4. Selected European Court of Justice direct tax cases

Year	Case	Name	Issue
1986	C-270/83	*Commission v. France (Avoir Fiscal)*	Imputation tax credit
1992	C-204/90	*Bachmann*	Taxation of workers;
	C-300/90	*Commission v. Belgium*	deductibility of insurance payments
1995	C-279/93	*Schumacker*	Taxation of workers
1997	C-28/95	*Leur-Bloem*	Tax avoidance
1997	C-250/95	*Futura Participations*	Cross-Border loss compensation
1998	C-264/96	*ICI v. Colmer*	Group/consortium relief
1999	C-307/97	*Saint-Gobain*	Treatment of branches
1999	C-200/98	*X AB and Y AB*	Domestic losses
2000	C-35/98	*Verkooijen*	Dividend exemption
2000	C-141/99	*AMID*	Cross border losses
2001	C-294/99	*Athinaiki*	Tax on distribution deemed a withholding tax
2001	C-397/98	*Metallgesellschaft*	Taxation of group income;
	C-410/98	*Hoechst*	Advance corporation tax
2002	C-324/00	*Lankhorst-Hohorst*	Thin capitalization
2003	C-168/01	*Bosal Holding BV*	Participation exemption; Parent/subsidiary Directive
2004	C-315-02	*Lenz*	Foreign dividends
2004	C-319/02	*Manninen*	Cross-border dividend imputation credit
Pending	C-446/03	*Marks & Spencer*	Group relief; cross-border loss compensation
Pending	C-196/04	*Cadbury Schweppes*	Anti-deferral and controlled foreign corporation regimes
Pending	C-492/04	*Lasertec*	Thin capitalization and non-EU countries

Source: European Commission (2005a).

the ECJ for relief. As a result, the European Court of Justice has effectively joined (some might say it has replaced) the European Commission in shaping EU company tax policy.

The ECJ's influence stems, in part, from the fact that it treats the European Union as a single jurisdiction rather than as a collection of individual Member States.[15] As a result, the Court tends to focus on determining whether an EU Member State's tax policies violate the fundamental freedoms in the EU Treaty.

Although the ECJ has always had this role, its actions are relatively recent, as it was not until 1986 in the *Avoir Fiscal* case that the ECJ issued its first major decision in the company tax area. In this case, the Court ruled that aspects of the French dividend imputation system violated the Treaty. Table 4 lists some key European Court of Justice decisions in direct taxation.

Many of the tax policies that the ECJ finds incompatible with the EU Treaty form a long-standing part of Member State company tax policies. These policies fall in the area of dividend imputation systems, rules restricting deductions for debt financing (thin capitalization rules), group relief provisions and cross-border loss compensation, exit taxes, and anti-deferral (controlled foreign corporation) measures.

The *Marks & Spencer* case illustrates one critical aspect of the problem. Marks & Spencer, plc, a U.K. corporation, incurred losses in the German, Belgian and French subsidiaries it held indirectly through a Dutch holding company. These subsidiaries had no economic activity in the United Kingdom.

Marks & Spencer claimed that it was entitled to offset the losses incurred by these subsidiaries against its U.K. taxable profits for the corresponding tax years. Under the United Kingdom's group relief provisions, however, a company may offset domestic profits with losses from foreign branches but not with losses from foreign subsidiaries. Marks & Spencer argued that by denying relief for losses in its EU subsidiaries, the U.K. tax legislation made it less attractive to establish subsidiaries in other Member States.

In April 2005, ECJ Advocate General Miguel Poiares Maduro issued an opinion supporting Marks & Spencer. He found that the U.K. law created an obstacle to cross-border investment and, thus, violated the Treaty's freedom of establishment provisions.[16]

The basic thrust of these decisions is clear: EU Member States have the right to set their own company tax policies, but they may not interfere with the Treaty's fundamental freedoms, particularly with the freedom of establishment. Member States may not discriminate against cross-border activity. Member States may not favor domestic investment over foreign investment. Member States may not restrict companies from establishing operations in another Member State.

The cumulative impact of these decisions is that Member States have de facto lost their sovereignty to set company tax policy independent of how those policies affect the functioning of the Single Market. As Advocate General Poiares Maduro noted:

"There is no doubt that the Member States as a matter of principle retain extensive competences in tax matters. However, they can no longer disregard the constraints imposed on their activities. They must endeavor to ensure that the choices made in tax matters take due account of the consequences which may flow therefrom for the proper functioning of the internal market."

The Advocate General all but called for action at the EU level. He concludes his opinion by noting that "it is not for the Court to determine a uniform scheme for all the Member States, basing its model on one national tax system or another or on a proposal that may be adopted by the Community institutions."

The ECJ is having a positive impact by removing cross-border tax obstacles in the European Union one by one. This process is a slow, but steady, way to eliminate the barriers to cross-border investment in the EU. However, this process may lead to 25 different ways of eliminating these tax barriers. For example, in response to the *Lankhorst-Hohorst* decision, Germany extended its thin capitalization rules to apply to domestic and foreign affiliates. Spain pursued the opposite course and extended its domestic exemption to the EU.

Taken individually, each Member State's policy may be compatible with the EU Treaty. But, taken as a whole, the collective impact of these policies may not help the EU meet its objective of becoming the "most competitive and dynamic knowledge-based economy in the world."[17]

2.5   COMMON CONSOLIDATED CORPORATE TAX BASE WORKING GROUP

The European Commission recognizes the importance of taking positive action in this area. It laid the foundation for implementing its company tax strategy in September 2004 when the Commission gained approval from a large majority of the Member States to pursue its short-term and long-term goals. The Commission then established the Common Consolidated Corporate Tax Base Working Group (CCCTB WG) as the forum for work on the common EU-level tax base.[18]

The Working Group will seek first to define the rules for calculating a common tax base without consolidation. These rules include structural elements of the tax base, such as rules governing depreciation, inventory valuation, treatment of expenses, and inter-company dividends.

The Working Group will then focus on additional issues relating to creating a common tax base with consolidation. These issues include the method of consolidation, the treatment of profits and losses, and the legal and administrative framework. Other important areas the Group will discuss include whether the entire scheme should be optional or whether individual elements of the tax base may be optional.

The Commission notes that devising an appropriate "apportionment mechanism" to distribute the tax base to the Member States forms a critical part of the comprehensive tax reform. Work on the apportionment mechanism will proceed simultaneously with work on the tax base, although the Commission has not yet established a formal means to take this work forward.[19]

The goal of the next three chapters is to advance that process by evaluating how formulary apportionment may operate in the European Union. Chapter 3 explains how formulary apportionment works. Chapter 4 evaluates issues concerning how to choose the factors for distributing the tax base across the Member States. Chapter 5 addresses related issues concerning the taxable connection, the tax base, and the taxable group.

Notes

1. Belgium, the Netherlands, Luxembourg, France, Germany and Italy signed the Treaty establishing the European Economic Community in Rome in 1957. For the latest version of the EU Treaty, see the *Official Journal of the European Communities*, C 325/33, 24 December 2002. The European Community became known as the European Union through the Maastricht Treaty on European Union in 1993.

2. See Gorter and de Mooij (2001).

3. See European Commission (2000).

4. Member States take into account other countries' tax systems through their bilateral tax treaties and in methods adopted to alleviate double taxation.

5. Austria and Italy adopted worldwide consolidation after the Commission released its study. France also offers worldwide consolidation, but in extremely limited cases.

6. As stated in the OECD Transfer Pricing Guidelines (1995), Article 9(1) of the OECD Model Tax Convention provides the authoritative statement of the arm's length principle. Article 9(1) provides that in the case of associated enterprises "[When] conditions are made or imposed between ... two [associated] enterprises in their commercial or financial relations which differ from those which would be made between independent enterprises, then any profits which would, but for those conditions, have accrued to one of the enterprises, but, by reason of those conditions, have not so accrued, may be included in the profits of that enterprise and taxed accordingly."

7. Although transfer pricing is typically viewed as an issue concerning cross-border transfers, some EU Member States require companies to apply the transfer pricing rules and regulations to solely domestic transactions. For example, as of 2005, Danish companies must comply with the disclosure and documentation requirements for transactions between Danish companies. Since 2004, the United Kingdom has required UK companies to comply with the transfer pricing rules for intercompany transactions between UK resident companies.

8. The United Kingdom may be an exception. According to the UK Inland Revenue (2005), transfer pricing manipulation had started to be a concern before the First World War and "remedial legislation" was first attempted in 1915, but the UK did not enact transfer pricing legislation (which later became ICTA88/S770) until 1951. By contrast, in 1928 the United States incorporated the predecessor to current Internal Revenue Code section 482 (as Section 45). See U.S. Department of the Treasury (1988). In 1939, the Department of Finance in Canada passed transfer pricing legislation as Section 23B of the 1939 Income Tax Act, although it was not until 1972 that Canada adopted arm's length pricing (Section 69) as part of the Tax Reform Package and not until 1976 that transfer pricing issues first became a major concern in Canada. For details on the Canadian history, see Eden, Dacin, and Wan (2001). The fact that a country has arm's length pricing rules and regulations, however, does not mean that the tax authorities enforce their legislation to the same degree. There is no doubt that the United States is in the forefront in enforcing the transfer pricing rules.

9. This "relaxed" attitude may exist in Ireland, where only a minority of Irish respondents believes that tax revenue authorities are paying increased attention to transfer pricing issues. Of course, with the low tax rate in Ireland, the Irish tax base is less vulnerable to income shifting than are the tax bases in countries that have higher tax rates. The lower the tax rate, the lower the benefit to transfer pricing manipulation.

10. If the home country exempts foreign-source income, a multinational company always has an incentive to shift income to the low tax jurisdiction. If the home country applies a foreign tax credit system, then the incentive depends on the company's foreign tax credit position and the ability to defer home country taxes. Since the EU plans to limit the new tax system to the EU's territorial boundaries, it will need to address the incentive to shift income out of the EU. I am grateful to Joseph Guttentag for emphasizing the importance of the foreign income issue.

11. Not all income shifting is inappropriate or inconsistent with arm's length pricing. Companies may shift income by applying arm's length prices within the range of acceptable arm's length prices.

12. The Commission Study (2002) reports that double taxation is a serious obstacle to the Internal Market. EU companies have recourse to the EU Arbitration Convention (see 90/436/EEC) to attempt to resolve such transfer pricing disputes.

13. See Copenhagen Economics (2004) for estimates of how company tax harmonization may affect EU welfare. See Wilson (1999) for evidence showing that tax competition has both benefits and drawbacks.

14. The Member States adopted the first measures in direct company taxation in July 1990. These measures include the merger directive (90/434/EEC), the parent/subsidiary directive (90/435/EEC) and the EU Arbitration Convention (90/436/EEC). In June 2003, the Member States approved the savings directive (2003/48/EC) and the interest and royalties directive (2003/49/EC).

15. The EU Treaty grants the European Court the primary role of interpreting EU law and ensuring that the EU Member States apply the law uniformly within the Community. Provisions in the EU Treaty take precedence over Member State law.

16. See Opinion of Advocate General Poiares Maduro delivered on 7 April 2005 in *Marks & Spencer plc. v. David Halsey (HM Inspector of Taxes)*, Case 446-03. See Sheppard (2005) and Martin (2004) for analyses of potential impacts on the Member States from the Marks & Spencer case.

17. See Lisbon European Council, 23 and 24 March 2000, Presidency conclusions.

18. For a description of the Working Group's program and objectives, see the various papers available on the website of the European Commission's Taxation and Customs Union. See http://europa.eu.int/comm/taxation_customs/taxation/index_en.html.

19. In March 2004, the European Commission invited tax experts from the academic world to a Workshop to examine details of a potential apportionment formula. The participants did not make any specific recommendations, but they came to consensus on some points. First, it is necessary to define clear criteria for evaluating an appropriate apportionment mechanism, and it is necessary to balance economic rationale with political acceptability. The participants preferred a formula based on a firm's particular characteristics to a formula based on macroeconomic factors, and they agreed that the system should be limited to the European Union's territorial borders, that is, to the EU water's edge.

Chapter 3

FORMULARY APPORTIONMENT IN THE EUROPEAN UNION

Growing pressures from the European Commission and the European Court of Justice to eliminate barriers to cross-border investment within the European Union may have convinced the individual Member States to transform how they tax EU multinational enterprises. Adopting common consolidated base taxation with formulary apportionment is one transformation under consideration. That transformation raises two questions: First, how should the apportionment formula be defined? Second, how should the EU-level tax base and taxable group be defined?

The next two chapters focus on the first issue: how to define the apportionment formula. Chapter 3 illustrates how formulary apportionment works and uses European data to illustrate how formulary apportionment might distribute income across the European Union. Chapter 4 draws from the experiences in the U.S. states and Canadian provinces to analyze some of the technical and practical issues concerning the composition of the formula and the apportionment factors.

The Common Consolidated Corporate Tax Base Working Group has already started work defining the technical elements of the EU-level tax base. Rather than duplicate those efforts, chapter 5 discusses issues related to introducing formulary apportionment: Nexus, the tax base, and the taxable group.

3.1 AN INTRODUCTION TO FORMULARY APPORTIONMENT

The basic idea of formulary apportionment is to assign income to the jurisdictions where a multijurisdictional company conducts its business activity.

If a company conducts twenty percent of its total activity in a jurisdiction, for example, then it apportions twenty percent of its total income to that jurisdiction. A typical apportionment formula distributes income to the location of a company's factories and employees and where it makes its sales and earns its gross receipts.

All of the U.S. states that tax corporate income and all of the Canadian provinces use a formula to distribute profits to the states and provinces, respectively.[1] A typical U.S. state formula, for example, distributes total income according to the share of total property, payroll, and sales in a state. The Canadian provinces distribute total income according to the share of total payroll and sales in each province.

Illustration of formulary apportionment

This section illustrates how formulary apportionment operates under the general formulae in the U.S. states and Canadian provinces.[2]   Many U.S. states apply a three-factor formula that weights the sales factor by one-half and weights the capital and payroll factors by one fourth, each. This formula is referred to as the "State" formula. State profits equal:

State Profits   =   [¼*(property in state/total property) +
                        ¼*(payroll in state/total payroll) +
                        ½*(sales in state/total sales)]
                        * total profits

Under this formula, which is also known as the double-weighted sales formula, the weight on the sales factor is twice the weight on the property and payroll factors.[3]

All of the Canadian provinces apply a payroll and sales formula with each factor weighted by one-half. This formula is referred to as the "Canadian" formula. Provincial profits equal:

Provincial Profits   =   [½*(payroll in province/total payroll) +
                        ½*(sales in province/total sales)]
                        *total profits

Table 5 shows a simple example of how formulary apportionment distributes a multinational company's income across two countries, A and B.[4] The top portion of the table shows a sample distribution of property, payroll and sales for a company doing business in two countries. Total income is assumed to be $1,000, and the multinational company reports $700 to Country A and $300 to Country B under separate accounting.

Table 5. Income Distribution under Formulary Apportionment

Factor	Country A	Country B	Total
Property	$3,000	$4,000	$7,000
Payroll	3,000	2,000	5,000
Sales	6,000	2,000	8,000
Taxable income under separate accounting	$700	$300	$1,000

Scenarios			Income
1. Both countries use the Canada formula (payroll + sales)			
A	$[½(3/5) + ½(2/5)]* 1,000$	=	675
B	$[½(2/5) + ½(3/5)]* 1,000$	=	325
Total			$1,000
2. Both countries use the State formula (property + payroll + 2 * sales)			
A	$[¼(3/7) + ¼(3/5) + ½(6/8)]* 1,000$	=	632
B	$[¼(4/7) + ¼(2/5) + ½(2/8)]* 1,000$	=	368
Total			$1,000
3. Each country adopts the revenue maximizing formula.			
A	$[½(3/5) + ½(2/5)]* 1,000$	=	675
B	$[¼(4/7) + ¼(2/5) + ½(2/8)]* 1,000$	=	368
Total			$1,043
4. Each country adopts the economic development formula.			
A	$[¼(3/7) + ¼(3/5) + ½(6/8)]* 1,000$	=	632
B	$[½(2/5) + ½(3/5)]* 1,000$	=	325
Total			$957

The first two scenarios assume that the two countries adopt the same apportionment formula. Scenario 1 shows the income distribution under the "Canada" formula and scenario 2 shows the income distribution under the "State" formula. The Canada formula distributes 67.5 percent of total income to Country A, while the State formula distributes 63.2 percent of total income to Country A. Thus, on a simple "revenue-maximizing" basis, Country A tax authorities prefer the "Canada" formula to the "State" formula. Country B tax authorities have the opposite preference.

Any uniform formula distributes exactly one hundred percent of income across locations, but one formula does not produce a "better" distribution than the other formula. Reconciling the divergent interests of the Member States in defining an apportionment formula is one of the many challenging tasks facing the European Union.

Scenarios 3 and 4 show the income distributions that arise when the two countries adopt different formulae. Scenario 3 shows the outcome if each country adopts the formula that it perceives maximizes its revenue. Scenario 4 shows the outcome if each country adopts the formula that it perceives promotes its economic development objectives. If locations use different formulae, then only in special situations (e.g., factor ratios are identical across locations) will 100 percent of a multistate company's total income be apportioned across the states.

In scenario 3, Country A adopts the Canadian formula and Country B adopts the State formula. Country A receives 67.5 percent of income and Country B receives 36.8 percent of income, for a total of 104.3 percent of income apportioned. The company's total income is over-apportioned in the sense that the post-apportionment tax base is greater than the pre-apportionment total tax base. Countries could eliminate the resulting double taxation by offering credits for the other country's tax. Failure to reconcile these differences might result in the multinational company suffering unrelieved double taxation. (In a dynamic setting, companies may re-allocate their investment away from the country with a relatively heavy weight on property. See chapter 7.)

Under-apportionment is also a possible outcome as countries compete for investment by adopting what may be referred to as an economic development formula.

Scenario 4 illustrates a case where countries pursue an economic development objective, that is, they reduce the weight on investment and/or employment within the country. In this case, country A adopts the State formula and country B adopts the Canada formula. Country A now claims 63.2 percent of income and Country B 32.5 percent of income for a total of 95.7 percent of total income apportioned. Income is under-apportioned. This example shows only the income distribution and not the tax burden, which depends on each country's tax rates. Suppose country A does not have an income tax. Then the company's total tax burden would be lower under scenario 3 than under scenario 4, despite the over-apportionment in scenario 3.

Table 5 has a further implication. Under no scenario does the hypothetical income distribution under formulary apportionment replicate the hypothetical income distribution under separate accounting. This situation highlights a critical point --- there is no reason to expect the income distribution under the two different methods to be identical. The table does not show that one outcome is the "correct" outcome. Formulary apportionment and separate accounting are two correct, but different ways to distribute taxable income.[5]

Finally, the table shows the incentives for a country to move to formulary apportionment and away from the current method. Country A's income is always higher under separate accounting than under either formula; Country B's income is always higher under formulary apportionment than under separate accounting. Putting this scenario in the EU context suggests that some Member States may be eager to move to formulary apportionment, while others may be reluctant to make such a move, regardless of the formula the European Commission may propose. In this situation, which may arise in the European Union since the Commission has proposed making formulary apportionment optional for Member States, the Member State tax authorities will need to find a means to reconcile the double taxation that may arise under the two, equally correct income allocation systems.

The above examples have several important implications. First, the EU Member States should adopt the same apportionment formula. Second, there is no single formula that will be appropriate in all cases for all countries, for all objectives, and at all times.[6] Third, there is no reason to expect the income distribution under formulary apportionment to replicate the income distribution under separate accounting. Finally, neither the outcome under separate accounting nor the outcome under formulary apportionment represents the "correct" income distribution. The two methods are merely different ways to assign income across locations.

3.2 ILLUSTRATIONS USING EUROPEAN UNION DATA

Using simple calculations, table 5 shows some potential implications of using formulary apportionment in the European Union. This next section uses actual data to provide a sharper picture of how formulary apportionment might distribute income, first from the perspective of the Member States overall and then from the perspective of one EU multinational enterprise.

Potential income distribution using employment shares

Table 6 illustrates how income might be distributed across the EU using a formula that distributes income according to the share of employees in each Member State. If employment is the only apportionment factor, this distribution also represents the share of total income each Member State would receive under this apportionment formula.

These data show that under a single-factor employee share formula, Germany receives 20 percent of income, and the United Kingdom, Italy, and France about 12 to 14 percent, each. Thus, four Member States receive about 60 percent of EU profits. This distribution suggests that the other twenty-one Member States may be interested in considering other factors to balance this employment factor. Sales, for example, are a good candidate since sales tend to be more widely distributed than manufacturing operations.

It is important to emphasize that the above table does not illustrate how formulary apportionment would distribute income across the Member States. The number of employees is not likely to be the only factor the EU includes in its apportionment formula. Furthermore, these data encompass all employees, not just those employed by multinational enterprises. An apportionment formula would only include employees working for multinational enterprises.

Table 6. Distribution of employees across the EU Member States, Q2-2002

	Share of Employees (%)		Share of Employees (%)
Austria	2.09%	Latvia	0.44%
Belgium	2.06	Lithuania	0.62
Cyprus	0.17	Luxembourg	0.09
Czech Republic	2.73	Malta	0.08
Denmark	1.31	Netherlands	3.75
Estonia	0.32	Poland	6.40
Finland	1.20	Portugal	2.64
France	11.77	Slovakia	1.15
Germany	19.63	Slovenia	0.51
Greece	1.92	Spain	9.07
Hungary	2.11	Sweden	2.08
Ireland	0.94	U.K.	14.68
Italy	11.78		

Source: Eurostat (2003), European Business Facts and figures, 1998-2002.

The distribution may not represent the actual employee distribution that would be considered when calculating the labor factor.

An illustration from a European multinational enterprise

EU multinational companies may be interested in how their tax liability may be affected by a move to formulary apportionment. This section provides an idea of a possible income distribution by drawing a picture from one EU multinational company using a formula with factors similar to those used in the U.S. states.

Unilever describes itself in its annual report as a "truly multi-local Multinational." Since 1930 when the Unilever group was formed, its two parent companies, Unilever NV and Unilever PLC, along with their group companies have operated as nearly as practicable as a single entity (the Unilever Group).

Regional figures in Unilever's annual report show the distribution of potential apportionment factors between Europe and the rest of the world.[7] Table 7 shows Unilever's financial statement pre-tax operating profits for Europe from 2000 to 2004. It also shows the share of Unilever's employees, turnover, and net operating assets in Europe for those same years. The number of employees stands for the payroll factor, turnover for the sales factor, and net operating assets for the property factor.

Using these financial statement figures as proxies for the apportionment factors, the table illustrates potential distributions of Unilever's profits under four different formulae: (1) property and payroll; (2) payroll and sales; (3) equally-weighted property, payroll and sales (the Massachusetts formula); and

Table 7. Illustration of factor and income distribution under apportionment from Unilever

	2004	2003	2002	2001	2000
A. Pre-tax operating profits in EUR millions					
Europe	€1,827	€2,563	€1,598	€2,412	€1,642
Share in Europe	53.6%	46.7%	31.9%	48.8%	52.5%
B. Shares in Europe					
Net operating assets (property)	46.6%	45.4%	43.6%	34.9%	35.7%
Employees (payroll)	23.3	23.5	24.3	26.8	27.1
Turnover (sales)	43.1	42.6	40.5	39.1	39.9
C. Share of income distributed to Europe under formulary apportionment					
(1) Property + Payroll	35.0%	34.4%	34.0%	30.9%	31.4%
(2) Payroll + Sales	33.2	33.1	32.4	32.9	33.5
(3) Three factor	37.7	37.2	36.2	33.6	34.2
(4) Double-weighted sales	39.0	38.5	37.3	35.0	35.6
D. Income apportioned to Europe in EUR millions:					
(1) Property + Payroll	€1,193	€1,888	€1,701	€1,526	€984
(2) Payroll + Sales	1,133	1,814	1,623	1,628	1,048
(3) Three factor	1,285	2,038	1,811	1,661	1,072
(4) Double-weighted-sales	1,331	2,113	1,865	1,729	1,116

Notes: Net operating assets are used for the property factor, number of employees for the payroll factor, and group turnover (sales of goods and services after deduction of discounts and sales taxes) for the sales factor. Net operating assets are the total of goodwill and intangible assets of subsidiaries, joint ventures and associates purchased after January 1, 1998, tangible fixed assets, stocks (inventory), debtors (excluding deferred taxation) less trade and other creditors and provisions for liabilities and charges. Turnover comprises Group turnover plus the Group share of turnover of joint ventures, net of the Group share of any sales to the joint ventures already included in the Group figures, but does not include the share of the turnover of associates. Turnover is stated on the basis of origin. Operating profit comprises Group operating profit plus the share of operating profit of joint ventures. The measure does not include the share of the operating profit of associates. Financial figures are in millions of euros.

The four apportionment formulae are defined as follows: (1) The property and payroll formula weights each factor by one-half. (2) The payroll and sales formula weights each factor by one-half. (3) The three factor "Massachusetts" formula weights property, payroll, and sales by one-third, each. (4) The double-weighted sales formula weights sales by one-half and property and payroll by one-fourth, each.

Source: Data are reported as part of the five-year record for the Unilever Group. See Unilever Annual Report, 2004.

(4) double-weighted sales (sales are weighted by one-half, and property and payroll are weighted by one-fourth, each).

In 2004, Europe accounted for nearly 54 percent of Unilever's worldwide pre-tax profits. Under formulary apportionment, however, the share reported in Europe that year ranges from 33 percent with a payroll and sales formula to 39 percent with a double-weighted sales formula.

Table 7 also shows a large difference between the share of income reported in Europe in the financial statements and the share of income apportioned to Europe under the four formulae. In all cases but one, the share under apportionment is substantially lower than the share using the financial accounts. The formulary method never apportions more than 39 percent of income to Europe. Except for the year 2002, when the European share of operating profits fell below 32 percent of the total, the financial statements never attribute less than 47 percent of total operating profits to Europe.

The income distribution attributed to Europe is relatively more stable under the formulary apportionment method than under the financial statement method. The percentage of income apportioned to Europe under any single formula never varies by more than five percentage points over this period (e.g., the share of income ranges from 35 percent to 39 percent with the double-weighted sales formula). By contrast, the share attributed to Europe in the financial statements ranges from a low of 32 percent in 2002 to a high of nearly 54 percent in 2004.[8]

As with the aggregate EU employee data from *Eurostat* used in Table 6, these data from Unilever's financial statements are only illustrative. The values used as the apportionment factors may not resemble the factors that the European Union may use in its apportionment formula. It is also important to stress that financial statement data are not tax data. The above table does not illustrate what Unilever's European profits would be under formulary apportionment; the table merely shows a possible distribution of worldwide income to Europe using publicly-available figures from the financial statements.[9]

3.3 SOME ADVANTAGES AND DISADVANTAGES

Advocates of formulary apportionment often present the system as a deceptively simple means to distribute a common tax base across the EU Member States. To balance these arguments, this section addresses the advantages and then the disadvantages of formulary apportionment.

Advantages of formulary apportionment

Formulary apportionment has many advantages. When applied on a consolidated basis, formulary apportionment generally restricts the ability of companies to re-locate their income by shifting income and expenses among related entities. Since the formula apportions total net income, a multinational enterprise can not alter its tax liability by moving profits from one related entity to another.

Using a formula to distribute the EU-level tax base to the individual Member States avoids the need to re-calculate income and expenses on a transaction-by-transaction basis to determine the amount of income earned in each individual Member State. Determining the geographic source of income and expenses becomes very difficult in a highly integrated economy. As long as the formula contains factors that represent where a company earns its income, it achieves a reasonably fair and equitable distribution of income based on where the companies actually do business.

When applied on a consolidated basis at the EU level, formulary apportionment treats an EU multinational company as an EU enterprise. It no longer requires a highly-integrated company to proceed on the basis that it is dealing with hypothetically separate entities on an arm's length basis. It provides a simple way to implement the European Commission's long-range company tax strategy.

If it is applied on a reasonably uniform basis, formulary apportionment operates very smoothly. Much of the relative lack of controversy in Canada is due to several features that distinguish its apportionment system from the system in the U.S. states. The most important reasons arise from the general uniformity of the provincial apportionment formula and the tax base. As a result, there have been few disputes over double taxation that arises from overlapping tax formulae or in tax bases. In addition, international controversy is largely avoided since the provincial income tax is basically restricted to Canadian income.

Formulary apportionment can greatly reduce compliance costs. It merely requires knowledge of total income and the apportionment factors in each location. In the European Union, a company theoretically would have to make just one calculation for the tax base and, supposing the EU uses the Massachusetts formula, three calculations for total property, payroll, and sales and one calculation for each of these factors in each Member State where it does business to distribute its income across locations. If a company operated in every EU Member State, it would calculate one tax base, three apportionment factor denominators, and 75 apportionment factor numerators. Fewer than 80 total calculations would be necessary. By contrast, when an EU company expands its operations into another EU Member State under the current system, it must compute its income under separate entity accounting and apply transfer prices to its cross-border internal transactions.

Finally, with the introduction of profit-based transfer pricing methods, EU multinational enterprises have become familiar with using formulae to distribute profits. Formulary apportionment is now more acceptable than it once was.

Disadvantages of formulary apportionment

Formulary apportionment has its disadvantages. An important issue concerns the ability of countries to reach agreement on the apportionment formula. Different formulae provide different income distributions, and no single apportionment formula is theoretically correct. It is not possible to design a formula that will replicate the current income distribution under separate accounting.

Even if the system is limited to the EU's territorial boundaries, multinational enterprises with operations outside the European Union will need to continue to apply the arm's length principle and tax authorities will continue to enforce the arm's length principle. EU Member States will need to develop measures to protect the EU tax base.[10]

The transfer pricing issue does not disappear within the EU. Multinational companies may "shift" income by relocating apportionment factors. This issue can be addressed, however, through the definition of the factor and is not an inherent "flaw" of apportionment.

On a technical matter, the distribution of income using a common formula may not reflect geographical variations in factor productivity. The mechanics of using a formula to distribute income imply that the factors in each location are equally productive. That is, one euro of capital in Ireland generates as much income as one euro of capital in Belgium.

Financial data, however, suggest that enterprises earn different rates of return across locations. For example, data reported by *Eurostat* (2001) indicate that foreign direct investment into Finland, Portugal, and the Netherlands was the most profitable among the EU countries in the late 1990s. Unilever reports wide variation in operating margins across geographical segments and over time. During the four quarters of 2004, Unilever's operating margin in Europe fluctuated from nearly 20 percent to a low of 5 percent while its operating margin in the Americas fluctuated between positive 17 percent and negative 17 percent over that same time period.

These differences should be eliminated in the long-run as profit maximizing companies relocate their investment until rates of return are equalized across locations. Nevertheless, variations in rates of return may exist for sustained periods in the short-term, and formulary apportionment may attribute income to locations where it was not earned while this dis-equilibrium exists.

As long as EU countries are not economically integrated, these location-specific productivity differences are likely to exist. No matter how much integration occurs, differences in rates of return will continue to exist. For example, Kroppen (2004) finds that the variability in company profits across the EU Member States is roughly comparable to the variation across the regions in the United States. The important question then becomes how precise the result from apportionment needs to be, that is, when do the differences in rates of return become meaningful? These variations in rates of return may be well within an acceptable "margin of error" in the income distribution. The reduction in cross-border barriers to investment in the EU is likely to cause any location-specific profits to diminish as investment flows to its most profitable locations.

Applying a standard formula to a multinational conglomerate may distort the income distribution when the conglomerate is composed of a number of different lines of business. For example, suppose that a company operates a grocery store and a department store.[11] The former store turns over its inventory a hundred times a year while the department store has a turnover of about two to three times per year. The sales factor then assigns a greater share of total income to the grocery store operation than to the department store. While the importance of this issue falls when all countries consider the same group so that over-taxation in one country offsets under-taxation in another country, it is nevertheless an important issue to consider.[12]

Another disadvantage may arise in the EU if, as may occur under the enhanced cooperation procedure, some Member States continue to use separate accounting while others move to formulary apportionment. In these cases, EU tax authorities will apply different approaches to measure income in each Member State. There is a slight chance that the income distribution will be the same, but in the vast majority of cases, the income distribution will differ.[13] If different taxing jurisdictions assert the right to tax the same income but can not agree on the distribution of income, multinational enterprises will bear the burden of the double taxation that arises when tax authorities fail to reach agreement.[14]

Many of the disadvantages of formulary apportionment arise when it is applied on an uncoordinated basis. However, if EU Member States can reach agreement on the basic elements of formulary apportionment (meaning they agree to use the same formula and roughly the same tax base), then many of formulary apportionment's disadvantages disappear. Tax authorities merely need to compare how multinational enterprises measure the factors in each location to determine whether they report the same valuation to each location. In cases where tax authorities do not agree on the income distribution, multinational enterprises can turn to dispute resolution methods, such as the competent authority agreement or the arbitration convention.

Although the EU Member States have accepted the use of profit-based transfer pricing methods, the basic approach remains firm-specific and transaction based. Global formulary apportionment may be the next step along the continuum of transfer pricing methods, but it may be a step too far for the European Union to take at this time.

There are means to avoid some of the disadvantages of using a common formula for all industries. For example, the EU may adopt a procedure that allows companies to request a different formula or to measure factors differently if the standard formula is not appropriate. The EU may also allow companies to request to enter into a type of agreement (similar to those available under advanced pricing arrangements) to use a firm-specific formula. Hybrid approaches could also be developed. For example, a multinational enterprise could apply a customized formula to apportion profits within the basic "core" of operations and continue to use traditional arm's length methods for operations that are outside of the core group.[15]

Finally, although the mechanical aspect of using a standard formula to distribute net income across locations is often presented as a drawback to the method, perhaps that aspect should, instead, be viewed as a benefit. A standard formula provides certainty to taxpayers and avoids the complexities that arise from attempting to fine tune the formula. The benefits from simplifying EU company taxation in this manner may very well outweigh the drawbacks of making a rough, but fair, distribution of income across countries.[16] Chapter 4 addresses this issue.

Notes

1. Five U.S. states do not have a corporate income tax. To focus on formulary apportionment, this example ignores many issues, such as the alleviation of double taxation that countries would need to address. It also defers a discussion of the factors and their definitions until chapter 4. It also defers discussion of issues concerning nexus, the tax base definition, and the taxable group until Chapter 5.

2. Canada refers to its system as formulary allocation. For ease of exposition, the text uses the term "formulary apportionment" to refer to the process of using a formula to distribute income across locations. This terminology is adopted to avoid confusion with the U.S. state practice of using "allocation" to refer to the process of assigning items of income to a specific location, rather than using a formula to apportion them to a location.

3. When referring to the double-weighted sales factor, it refers to a formula that weights the sales factor by one-half and the property and payroll factors by one-fourth, each. As of 2005, this formula is the most common formula used in the states. Not all states weight each factor equally, and some states exclude property and payroll from the formula.

4. For ease of exposition, the jurisdictions are referred to as countries.

5. The U.S. Supreme Court essentially reached this conclusion in the case concerning the constitutionality of the state worldwide combined reporting method in *Container Corp. v. Franchise Tax Board* (1983). The Court concluded that the U.S. states were not required to adopt the method of taxation adopted by the federal government. Both methods created the risk of double taxation. The risk of double taxation could be avoided if the jurisdictions that used separate accounting adopted the formulary apportionment method (and applied them in the same manner). Neither method avoids all risk of double taxation.

6. Country objectives may change over time. Whereas the U.S. states at one time may have designed their apportionment formula to maximize revenue, over time the objective become one of maximizing economic development incentives.

7. With more specific information, it would be possible to calculate distributions across particular European countries. The company may have the information needed to distribute its EU group income across the Member States. If the company were interested, it could use the typical apportionment factor definitions provided in Chapter 4 as an initial approach.

8. The same pattern holds in data going back to 1997, as shown in Unilever's 2001 annual report.

9. This point is highlighted by the difference in net income reported for U.S. GAAP purposes and under IFRS shown in Unilever's financial statements. Unilever reports €1,876 million in net profits in its consolidated profit and loss account in 2004. When converted to U.S. GAAP, net profit rises to €2,686 million. This difference emphasizes the point made earlier with respect to the different outcomes under separate accounting and formulary apportionment. The two measures of financial income are both "correct" as each figure merely represents the outcome under different accounting principles.

10. The work at the OECD on Transfer Pricing Guidelines will, thus, remain vital in working on developments in the transfer pricing area.

11. I am grateful to Ben Miller of the California Franchise Tax Board for providing this example.

12. See Miller (1995) for examples of how states deal with the issue of combining dissimilar businesses.

13. The difficulty in reaching agreement on the income distribution that results under two different allocation methods is often cited as a reason not to move to formulary apportionment in a world where separate accounting is the standard. For examples, see the arguments presented by the OECD (1995) in Chapter 3 of the revised Transfer Pricing Guidelines and the discussion of the U.S. Treasury Department conference on formulary apportionment in Fernandez (1996). If the EU Member States agree to move to formulary apportionment, however, this argument has less importance.

14. Although double taxation is the chief concern, the typical outcome may be under-taxation as multinational enterprises exploit the cross-border variations to minimize their taxes.

15. For details, see Amerkhail (2000)

16. As Rosenbloom (2005) finds, "[a]rm's length may well be the better of competing principles, but the contest is not quite the rout that the OECD and some of its members have described. . . . It is not only the formulary approach that suffers from flaws in theory, concept and method."

Chapter 4

THE APPORTIONMENT FORMULA

This chapter addresses the basic formula design issue for purposes of developing an idea on the shape a potential EU apportionment formula may take. From the outset, it is important to note that the apportionment formula does not need to follow the traditional practice of reflecting the characteristics of the company. The EU Member States may decide to distribute income using macroeconomic factors, such as per capita national income, or according to industry average factor ratios rather than according to firm-specific factors.

Since neither of these formulae uses firm-specific factors, they restrict a firm's ability to shift the location of the apportionment factors for tax purposes. However, by removing the connection between the company's income and its tax liability, both formulae raise important policy issues concerning the use of the corporate income tax as a revenue redistribution tool. An industry average formula provides a better match than a macroeconomic formula between the corporation and the apportionment factors.[1] However, it also raises the complication of determining to which industry a company belongs and whether a particular company's tax liability should depend on the industry average factor distributions.

Thus, a priori, the EU may wish to use a firm-specific formula that reflects where the company, itself, earns that income. However, the Member States may wish to keep these alternatives in mind.

This chapter focuses on issues relating to a formula that uses firm-specific factors.[2] The chapter first discusses how to choose the apportionment factors and then how to define the factors. This discussion centers on issues concerning the manufacturing and merchandising sector. A final section briefly addresses issues concerning the composition of a formula designed for other industries, such as transportation and financial industry.[3]

4.1   PRINCIPLES OF FORMULARY APPORTIONMENT

Preliminary issues

A few basic principles apply when considering how to design a firm-specific apportionment formula for the European Union. Many of these issues focus on how to design an efficient and equitable formula. As is the case in many areas of economic policy, it is generally not possible to achieve these goals simultaneously. An efficient formula may produce a less equitable outcome than a formula that is less efficient. The list below gives some indication of the considerations to take into account in designing a formula.

First, the formula should be politically acceptable to a wide range of EU Member States. A formula that does not appear to create a fair balance of the tax burden, either across sectors or between domestic and multinational enterprises, is less likely to be acceptable than a formula that tries to reach such a balance.

Closely related to the above point is that the formula should take a range of factors into consideration. A formula that overly weights one factor or that ignores another factor may not produce an acceptable income distribution compared with a multiple-factor formula.

The formula should distribute income across the Member States according to sensible notions of where a company earns its income. The locations where a company has opened an office, hired employees, and made sales provide a good indication of the source of at least some of the company's business income.

Countering the above proposition, however, is the point that the formula should minimize the distortions to the location of business activity. Since the formula effectively acts as a tax on the factors in the formula (see chapter 7), it may discourage the use of those factors in a location. A formula that distributes income according to the location of a highly-mobile factor will become susceptible to manipulation and tax base erosion.

The formula should produce a relatively stable income distribution over time. A formula that includes multiple factors will be more stable over time than a single-factor formula.

Finally, the formula should include factors that are easily measured. Such a formula remains relatively simple in terms of taxpayer compliance and administrative feasibility.

These guiding principles provide a sound basis for considering how to design an apportionment formula. A review of the list, however, shows that no single formula can meet all of these goals simultaneously. For example, a factor that is easy to measure, such as number of employees, may not produce a desirable income distribution. Likewise, intangible property generates a significant amount of income for many companies, yet intangible property is both very difficult to measure and difficult to locate. Thus, it fails two of the basic design tests. The Canadian formula includes only two factors, yet it has produced few controversies. Therefore, the above list should be considered a guide for thinking about how to choose the apportionment factors.

Choosing the factors in theory

Economic theory provides considerable support for including certain factors in the apportionment formula.[4] For example, since corporate income reflects the return to capital, income should be apportioned on the basis of the location of capital.

While economic theory may suggest such a solution, political reality points to a different solution. Firms generate income through the use of both capital and labor. Thus, the apportionment formula should also reflect labor's contribution to that income.

A formula that apportions income according to the location of capital and labor conforms to the notion that jurisdictions have the right to tax income generated by the factors of production located in their jurisdiction. In other words, it recognizes the entitlement of the source state to tax factors located within its boundaries. A property and payroll formula assigns income according to its geographical source, i.e., the location of production.

The design features listed above, however, suggest that a formula that assigns income solely to production locations may not be widely acceptable. For example, suppose the EU has many companies that concentrate production in a few Member States and sell throughout the EU. If the EU adopts a formula that includes only payroll and property, that formula may not distribute income in a way that is acceptable to a wide range of Member States.

Thus, the location of sales, i.e., the marketing location, might be viewed as entitled to a share of the tax base. A formula that includes a sales factor with sales measured at destination assigns some income to the location of customers. To make the formula equitable, the EU may wish to take the interests of the marketing locations into consideration.[5]

Choosing the factors in practice

These guiding principles helped shape the development of the formula in the provinces and in the states. For example, as the U.S. states refined their apportionment formulae during the mid-20th century, they settled on the property, payroll, and sales formula as the desired common formula. In 1957, the states developed a set of uniform rules that provide for the three-factor equally weighted property, payroll, and sales formula (which was then commonly referred to as the "Massachusetts" formula).

By 1977, all but a few states used this formula.[6] As the U.S. Supreme Court explained, "the three-factor formula . . . has gained wide approval precisely because payroll, property, and sales appear in combination to reflect a very large share of the activities by which value is generated."[7]

The EU may be interested in the process that resulted in the general uniformity in the provincial formula and tax base. Since regaining the right to levy a provincial corporate income tax after WWII, the provincial apportionment formula and tax base have been essentially uniform across all the provinces. This outcome occurred through joint work with the federal government, and from the fact that many of the rules, for example, the permanent establishment rule, were substantially the same as those in the 1942 Canada-U.S. income tax convention.

The provinces recognized that they would need to develop an apportionment formula that would distribute income as fairly as possible across the provinces. Smith (1998) explains that reaching agreement on a fair and uniform formula was viewed as more important than dividing income across the provinces in exact proportions.

The provinces initially considered a formula based solely on gross receipts, but quickly settled on an equally-weighted payroll and sales formula to balance the interests of the larger and smaller provinces. As Smith (1976) explains: "Presumably, the designers of the rules felt that a single factor [gross receipts] formula might attribute too great a share of the corporation's profits to the province where its head office was located, and that an additional factor giving weight to the profit from activities performed in the province by its employees would better reflect reality. But there was, one can guess, no desire to get into the complications and controversies of a three-factor formula involving capital assets in the province."[8]

Since the early 1960s, the provinces have applied the same formula and there is little, if any, pressure on the provinces to deviate from this formula. Both taxpayers and the tax authorities value the administrative and compliance benefits that arise from the uniform apportionment formula.

Choosing factor weights

Although the factor weights are important, the choice of factor weights is essentially arbitrary. For example, if the formula contains two factors, as in Canada, it may be sensible to weight each factor evenly. The EU may wish to balance the weights applied to factors in the production and marketing locations. The "double-weighted sales formula" that weights sales by one-half and property and payroll by one-fourth, each, achieves such an objective. A formula that weights sales by one-half, payroll by one-third, and property by one-sixth, as Musgrave (2000) discusses, also reaches such a balance.

The double-weighted sales formula may have an advantage over the other formulae described since it maintains a balance on the weights applied to the capital and labor factors. However, by reducing the weight on capital (at the expense of eliminating the balance between capital and labor), the other formulae reduce the effective tax rate levied on capital, thus reducing the distortions to investment location. Chapter 7 addresses some of the empirical and theoretical issues surrounding the use of capital as an apportionment factor.

4.2 APPORTIONMENT FACTOR DEFINITIONS AND LOCATIONS

With the general principles established, this section turns to some technical issues related to the apportionment formula. Because the U.S. states and Canadian provinces have such a long experience with formulary apportionment, a good place to begin is with the formula and definitions in these locations. One obvious point to make is that regardless of how the factors are defined, the EU should measure the numerators and denominators of the factors in the same way across Member States.

In Canada, the Federal government agrees to incur the costs of administering the provincial tax in exchange for provincial agreement to adopt the federal definition of the payroll and gross receipts factors. Thus, the factors are defined identically across the provinces (this statement is true even in the provinces that have not entered into the agreements).

Due in large part to the influence of the Uniform Division of Income for Tax Purposes Act (UDITPA), which was written in 1957, the U.S. states use fairly similar definitions of the property, payroll and sales (gross receipts) factors.[9] UDITPA sets forth rules for dividing income into business income, which is apportioned using the equally-weighted property, payroll, and sales formula, and non-business income, which is allocated to specific states. UDITPA also provides definitions of the apportionment factors.

In considering how to define the factors, it should be kept in mind that the value of a factor is more reliable if its value is reported for purposes other than the apportionment formula. For example, the numerator of the U.S. state payroll factor is the amount of compensation reported to the federal government for unemployment compensation purposes. This independent use of payroll data improves the reliability of the payroll factor.

Most EU Member States have a common payroll measure readily available at the OECD. As part of preparing standardized figures across OECD member countries, the OECD (2003b) calculates standardized payroll figures. Thus, the EU may consider using this definition for the payroll factor. Similar common measures exist for value added, investment, production, and other potential apportionment factors.

To the extent that figures are obtained from financial statements that are audited or reported for other purposes, the values also will have an independent source for verification purposes. Many of the figures the states and provinces use in their apportionment formulae are also used for purposes of stock exchange filings, for example.

Definitions and locations of the factors

This section provides a simple description of how the states and provinces define and locate the apportionment factors. Since the state definitions vary, this section provides only a general idea of how they define and locate each factor.[10] This section also discusses Canadian definitions and locations for the payroll and gross receipts factors.

The numerator of the apportionment factor includes its value in the state (or province) for the taxable period and the denominator includes its value over all locations for the taxable period. (The definition of "all locations" depends on the scope of the taxable group.)

This section does not attempt to analyze the benefits and drawbacks of each of these factors, although a glance at the definitions below reveals some areas where the European Union may wish to modify the definitions.[11] For example, the standard state formula includes property at its original cost rather than at market value. The Canada formula does not include property.

In considering potential apportionment factors in addition to those described below, the EU may wish to focus on items that are available in a company's financial statements or that are reported for other purposes. With the introduction of International Financial Reporting Standards (IFRS), many EU multinational enterprises now have standard measures in each Member State of these potential apportionment factors. Likewise, the EU may with to coordinate the rules for determining the location of sales with rules that apply for the EU value added tax purposes.[12]

Property: The property factor includes land, buildings, machinery, equipment, inventories, and other real and tangible personal property. Property may include the value of movable property, such as tools, construction equipment and trucks, that are used within and without the state according to the share of total time spent in the state during the year.

Owned tangible property is valued at the basis of the property for federal income tax purposes at the time of acquisition. Property is adjusted for certain capital improvements and deductions, but not for depreciation. Rental property is valued at eight times its net annual rent.

Many of these values are obtained from the taxpayer's balance sheet. In general, the states do not include intangible property in the property factor.

The states generally assign real and tangible personal property to the state where the property is owned or rented and used during the tax period in the regular course of the taxpayer's trade or business. Property in transit may be assigned to the destination location or according to the amount of time spent in the state as a share of the total.

Payroll: Payroll is measured by employee compensation, including wages, salaries, commissions and any other form of remuneration paid or accrued to employees for personal services. Payroll may include compensation paid to executive officers and certain in-kind payments, such as the value of board, rent, housing, lodging, and other benefits or services. Payroll generally excludes payments made to independent contractors and others who are not classified as employees.

The states generally assign payroll to the location where it is assigned for federal unemployment insurance purposes. If an employee performs services in more than one state, payroll is assigned to the state where the employee's base of operations is located.

The Canadian payroll factor includes compensation and taxable benefits paid to employees. The provinces assign salaries and wages to the location of the permanent establishment where the employee normally reports to work. Salaries and wages for head office administration are assigned to the province where the head office is located.

Sales: The sales, or gross receipts, factor generally includes all gross receipts derived by the taxpayer from transactions and activity in the regular course of the trade or business. Sales include sales of tangible personal property and gross receipts from services and all other gross receipts, such as interest, dividends, rents, royalties, capital gains, and other income derived by the taxpayer in the regular course of business.

The location of sales and gross receipts depends on the type of sale or gross receipt.

The states assign receipts from tangible personal property sales to the destination state, that is, to the state where the property is shipped or delivered. Many states apply a "throwback" rule that returns sales to the state of origin if the sale is not taxable in the state of destination (or if the sale is to the U.S. Government). Some states apply a "throwout" rule that removes sales that do not have an identifiable location from the sales factor. The effect of the throwback rule is to distribute income according to sales in the origin state. The effect of the throwout rule is to distribute income according to the taxpayer's overall activities as measured by the other apportionment factors.

States generally assign receipts from sales of services to the state where the income-producing activity occurs. Some states assign receipts according to the ratio of time spent performing services in a state to the total time spent performing the services everywhere. Some states apply an "all or nothing" rule and assign all receipts from personal services to the state where the greater share of services is performed, based on costs of performance.

States generally assign sales of other than tangible personal property to the state where the property is located. If the property is mobile, the state may assign gross receipts to the state if the base of operations for the property is in the state. Gross receipts may be assigned according to the amount of time that the property is physically present or used within the state relative to the total amount of time or use of the property everywhere during the taxable year.

Special rules apply for assigning the location of receipts from intangible personal property. In cases where the location of the income-producing activity can be identified, the receipts are assigned to the location where that activity occurs. In cases where the income cannot be assigned to any particular income-producing activity, then it also cannot be identified with any specific location, and the receipts are excluded entirely from the sales factor.

Canada assigns gross receipts to the location where the receipts are "reasonably" considered to have been earned, which is based on the location of the permanent establishment. If the taxpayer does not have a permanent establishment in the other provinces or country where the customer is located, then the provinces employ a rule that assigns the receipts either to the location of production or manufacture or, if the merchandise was produced or manufactured in more than one province, to each province according to the salaries and wages paid to employees in each of the locations where the taxpayer has a permanent establishment involved in producing or manufacturing the merchandise.

Illustrations for the U.S. states and Canadian provinces

This next section illustrates how a taxpayer calculates the apportionment factors in the states and in the provinces.

For state tax purposes, a taxpayer computes its apportionment formula for each state in which it does business. A state taxpayer generally reports only the factor located in that particular state and the totals across all locations. For detailed descriptions of these practices, see the rules and regulations of a particular state (e.g., Franchise Tax Board, 2002a).

Table 8 illustrates a typical list of values included in the apportionment factors that a taxpayer reports on its state corporate income tax return. This list is merely illustrative as any particular state may request a different amount of detail. Depending on the definition of the group, any intercompany transactions are eliminated in calculating the apportionment factors.

Canada

Taxpayers follow a different process in calculating the provincial apportionment factors. A taxpayer doing business in more than one province reports the values for its apportionment factors for each province on the Federal form. As a result, the Canadian process ensures that the sum of the amounts reported across all of the provinces equals the overall total. By requiring taxpayers to report this information, Canada avoids the problems of inconsistent reporting that may arise in the U.S. states. In the U.S. states, by contrast, taxpayers file a different tax return for each state and, thus, may report different denominator totals in different states.[13]

Table 9 shows the Canadian process. This table replicates the form that taxpayers file for federal, provincial, and territorial tax purposes.

Table 8. Illustration of state apportionment formula

Factor	In-State Value	Total Value	State Share
Property Factor			
Inventories			
Land			
Furniture and fixtures			
Machinery and equipment			
Buildings			
Other assets			
Less: construction in progress			
Total owned property			
Eight times annual rental expense			
Total owned and rented property			
Payroll Factor			
Wages and salaries			
Compensation of officers			
Commissions and other compensation			
Total compensation			
Sales and Gross Receipts Factor			
Gross sales			
Less returns and allowances			
Dividends			
Interest			
Rents			
Royalties			
Gross capital gains			
Other			
Total sales and gross receipts			
Total of the three factors divided by three			
STATE APPORTIONMENT FACTOR			

4.3 FORMULAE FOR SPECIFIC INDUSTRIES

The typical apportionment formula developed for manufacturing and merchandising firms may not be appropriate for some industries as it may not include factors that generate income for that industry or the factor definitions may not be appropriate for that industry. For this reason, the states and provinces have developed different formulae for specific industries. These formulae generally take into consideration the importance of intangibles in certain industries, such as the financial industry, while other formulae take into consideration the mobility of the property factor, such as in the transportation industries.

Table 9. Illustration of apportionment calculation in Canada

Province	Wages ($)	Share (%)	Gross Sales ($)	Share (%)	Average Share (%)
Newfoundland and Labrador					
Prince Edward Island					
Nova Scotia					
New Brunswick					
Quebec					
Ontario					
Manitoba					
Saskatchewan					
Alberta					
British Columbia					
Northwest Territories					
Nunavut					
Yukon					
TOTAL					

Source: Modified from Schedule 5 Allocation of Taxable Income, Revenue Canada.

For example, many U.S. states apply specialized formulae that cover certain industries, such as construction contractors, airlines, railroads, trucking companies, television and radio broadcasting, and publishing.[14]

Financial institutions (e.g., a national or state bank, a bank holding company, or a savings and loan) generally calculate the payroll factor the same way as other corporations, but apply different definitions for the property and the gross receipts factor. Financial institutions include certain intangible property in the property factor and use a "receipts" factor instead of a "sales" factor. For example, the property factor may include intangible property, such as coin and currency, loans related to in-state property and credit card receivables if the fees and charges are billed to the state. Likewise, the receipts factor may include income from securities and money market instruments, interest income from loans secured by personal property in the state, and receipts from credit cards if regularly billed to the state.

Taxpayers involved in interstate transportation business may apply a formula that relates to a measure of "revenue miles" in the state. For example, an airline company may apportion its income solely on the basis of total revenue aircraft miles flown in the state compared to total miles flown everywhere.

If a single corporation is composed of businesses that use different apportionment formulae, then the apportionment formula that applies to the corporation depends on particular state practice. For example, a state may require a company to determine the appropriate formula to use depending on its predominant area of business, where the predominant business is measured according to the share of gross receipts earned in each business. In other cases, such as for insurance companies, a corporation may be determined to be an insurance company and thus required to use the formula for the insurance industry if the company is treated as an insurance company for purposes of the Internal Revenue Code.[15]

The need to determine the particular industry is less important if the number of different formula definitions is minimized (although, there are good reasons for providing specialized formulae for certain industries). Certain exceptions, of course, may always be necessary. For these purposes, U.S. state taxpayers have the "equitable relief" provision of Section 18 of UDITPA available. Thus, "if the allocation and apportionment provisions ... do not fairly represent the extent of the taxpayer's business activity in the state" a taxpayer may request to use another method to determine its state income, including separate accounting, exclusion or inclusion of a factor, or any other method. (The tax authority may require the taxpayer to use an alternative method in such cases as well.)

The U.S. federal government applies formulary methods in specific cases. For example, in certain advance pricing agreements with companies involved in global trading, taxpayers use a formula that distributes profits according to a value, a risk, and an activity factor.[16] In these cases, the factor definitions and their weights are specific to each firm, but the basic principle may be applied on a wider basis.

Canada provides specific apportionment formulae for nine industries --- insurance corporations, banks, trust and loan corporations, railway corporations, airline corporations, grain elevator operators, bus and truck operators, ship operators, and pipeline operators --- and for so-called divided businesses and nonresident corporations.[17] These formulae generally reflect a particular feature of that industry. For airline corporations, for example, a fixed asset cost factor replaces the payroll factor and a revenue plane miles flown factor replaces the gross receipts factor.

Insurance companies apportion their income entirely on the basis of the location of net premiums, and trust and loan corporations apportion solely on the basis of gross revenue. Banks apportion according to salaries and wages and the amount of loans and deposits in a province, and the loan factor is double weighted.

Special rules apply for divided businesses, that is, a corporation that conducts its business in more than one industry. In this case, the corporation and tax authority may agree on the appropriate formula to apply. This process may involve assigning a share of income according to the predominant business, as discussed above, and apportioning the remaining income according to the standard payroll and gross receipts formula.

Notes

1. See Robinson (2000) for a suggestion that industry-specific apportionment formulae could be designed that would avoid the "rough justice" of an arbitrary apportionment formula while also maintaining many of the administrative benefits of using a formula to distribute income across borders. See also Amerkhail (2000) for further details.

2. This section parallels the analysis in Weiner (2005).

3. Since state tax policies change frequently, this section merely describes some of the general state practices and does not attempt to provide a comprehensive analysis of current practices in all of the states. For such details, see Hellerstein and Hellerstein (1998, cum. Supp 2005).

4. Peggy Musgrave (1972, 1984, 2000) is one of the leading authors to address issues concerning interjurisdictional equity in company taxation. This issue arises in the case of company taxation when a company does business in more than one taxing location. The basic question becomes which jurisdiction has the entitlement to tax and how much of the tax base should be assigned to each jurisdiction. See Musgrave (2000) for a specific discussion of the idea of interjurisdictional equity in the European Union.

5. Musgrave (1984) explains that demand considerations could be taken into account under separate accounting by allowing sales activities to be considered in determining whether a permanent establishment exists. As discussed in chapter 5, multinational enterprises generally oppose basing the entitlement to levy an income tax on the presence of sales.

6. Iowa, as discussed later, was an important exception. It apportioned on the basis of destination-based sales only. Other states made other formulae, such as a double-weighted sales formula available, but Iowa was the only state to apportion on the basis of a single factor. The District of Columbia also used such a formula.

7. See *Container Corp. v. Franchise Tax Board*, 463 U.S 159 (1983). As discussed in chapter 7, twenty-five years later, the general uniformity in state apportionment formulae has disappeared as a growing number of states have moved toward a formula that weights sales disproportionately.

8. For additional details, see Smith (1998) and Perry (1989). Some of the special industry formulae, such as for insurance companies, banks, railways, and airlines, included a capital asset factor as long as the location and value of the assets could be established.

9. For a copy of UDITPA, see www.law.upenn.edu/bil/ulc/fnact99/1920_69/udiftp57.pdf. This discussion applies to the manufacturing and merchandising industry. Special formulae apply to other industries, as discussed later.

10. For details of specific state practices, see Hellerstein and Hellerstein (1998, cum supp. 2005), Healy (2001) and the Multistate Tax Commission Regulations (2003).

11. See McLure (2002) and Hellerstein and McLure (2004) for evaluations of these issues.

12. There are compelling reasons to apply consistent rules for assigning the location of certain sales, e.g., digital services, for value added tax and for income tax purposes. For further discussion, in the area of electronic commerce, see the "E-VAT" Directive, which establishes rules for determining the location of certain electronically-supplied services. Council Directive 2002/38/2003 entered into force on July 1, 2003.

13. As described in chapter 6, the joint audit program developed in the U.S. states attempts to ensure that taxpayers consistently report their apportionment factors across the states. As part of this process, taxpayers may be required to provide a "Domestic Disclosure Spreadsheet" where they report the factors and income reported to each state. The purpose of the spreadsheet is to ensure that the taxpayer does not report different amounts of property, payroll, or sales to the various states in which it does business. The Canadian form for calculating the provincial apportionment factors resembles this type of spreadsheet.

14. See MTC Regulations (2003).

15. See, for example, the Illinois Income Tax Act (35 ILCS 5/1501). See Miller (1995b) for a more general discussion.

16. See U.S. Internal Revenue Service Notice 94-40, 1994-1, C.B. 351. In these APAs, the IRS, the taxpayer, and the treaty partner agree that the taxpayer's global income should be distributed across countries using a profit split method. The formula contains three factors: a value factor, a risk factor, and an activity factor. The value factor is generally measured as compensation paid to traders in a location, the risk factor reflects the volume of swap transactions or open commodity positions, and the activity factor includes compensation paid to the support staff and the net present value of transactions executed in a trading location.

17. The general apportionment rules are in Regulation 402. Regulations 403 to 413 provide the apportionment rules for these specific industries. See also Schedule 5 of the tax return.

Chapter 5

NEXUS, THE TAX BASE AND THE TAXABLE UNIT

Nexus, the tax base, and the taxable unit are key elements of any company tax system. The methods the U.S. states and Canadian provinces use to address these issues often are similar to the methods countries have chosen to address these issues.

Concerning nexus, for example, for most categories of business profits, bilateral tax treaties concluded by OECD countries apply the permanent establishment concept to determine whether a non-resident entity has a taxable presence, or nexus, in the country. The Canadian provinces also apply the permanent establishment concept to determine whether a non-resident has a taxable connection in a province.

In terms of the tax base, countries distinguish between how they treat business income and how they treat non-business (investment) income. Countries frequently assign items of investment income to a particular jurisdiction according to a particular rule. The main differences arise in how countries and the U.S. states treat business income. The states distribute business income across locations using a formula. Countries distribute business profits across locations using separate accounting and source of income and expense rules.

A similar analysis applies for the taxable unit. Some countries, such as Canada, do not allow any form of consolidation. A handful of EU Member States also do not allow consolidation. Some countries, such as the United States, allow domestic consolidation, while some EU countries, such as Denmark and Italy, allow both worldwide and domestic consolidation.

5.1   NEXUS --- THE TAXABLE CONNECTION

This section discusses some tests that apply to determine when a non-resident has established a taxable connection.

Physical presence

In the United States, a U.S. state may tax only the income produced by a taxpayer's activities that have a substantial connection with the state. Physical presence beyond a *de minimis* amount is generally viewed as meeting the threshold. A non-resident company that has located its factories and employees in a state likely has a sufficient presence to be subject to that state's income tax. Taxable presence may also be established based on a non-resident's sales activity in the state.[1] Under general practices at the international level, however, if a non-resident's only presence in a jurisdiction is through its sales, it generally has not established a taxable connection for purposes of income taxation.[2]

Intangible or economic presence

Companies generate income through the use of not only physical factors, such as property and employees, but also from the use of their intangible property, such as patents, franchises, and trademarks. Out-of-state companies obtain significant benefits from "doing business" in a state even if they are not physically present within a state. It is unsettled at the state level whether physical presence is necessary to impose a state corporate income tax on a non-resident company.[3]

Many U.S. states have dealt with the issue of whether the presence of intangibles is sufficient to create a taxable connection with the state. This issue frequently arises when an out-of-state company licenses its trademarks or tradenames to an affiliate in the taxing state. The state asserts that the out-of-state entity, whose only presence in the state is through its intangible property, becomes subject to income tax in the states where its affiliates use its intellectual property.

A state case dealing with this issue arose in 1993. In this case, Geoffrey, Inc., a Delaware corporation, had no employees, offices, or tangible property in South Carolina or in any other state. Geoffrey had about $55 million of income but paid no income taxes to any state.[4] It earned most of its income from royalties it received from the use of its trademarks by the retail Toys 'R' Us stores located in South Carolina and elsewhere.

The South Carolina State Court ruled that the presence of Geoffrey's intangible property in the state created a constitutionally sufficient connection with the state. As the Court noted, "[T]he real source of Geoffrey's income is not a paper agreement, but South Carolina's Toys 'R' Us customers." Through the presence of its intangibles, Geoffrey became subject to South Carolina tax on the share of its royalty income apportioned to the state.[5]

Other state courts, however, have ruled that physical presence is necessary to create a taxable presence for the state corporate income tax. For example, in 2003, the New Jersey Tax Court found that a holding company was not subject to the state corporate income tax since its only presence in the state occurred through its intangibles.[6]

Indicating the unsettled nature of this issue, in 2005, the New Jersey Appellate Division concluded that physical presence is not necessary for a foreign corporation to be subject to the state corporate income tax.[7] This decision has important implications for the nexus standard. As Hellerstein and Hellerstein (1998, Cum Supp. 2005) explain, the New Jersey Appellate Division "repudiated the analysis of the New Jersey Tax Court that had momentarily stood as the leading decision defending the view that *Quill's* Commerce Clause 'substantial nexus' standard of physical presence applies to income taxes."

Hellerstein and Hellerstein (1998, Cum Supp. 2005) analyze the numerous judicial and administrative developments in this area since the *Geoffrey* decision in 1993 to determine if the states exhibit any trends concerning whether intangible presence creates nexus. They find that, although the developments are mixed, the reactions across the country generally support the view in *Geoffrey* that physical presence is not required for the state corporate income tax.

Permanent establishment

Canada applies the permanent establishment concept for nexus purposes. In general, if a corporation has a fixed place of business in the province it has a permanent establishment. A taxpayer with a permanent establishment in more than one province apportions its income across the provinces.[8] A corporation that transacts all of its business from outside the province through mail order and catalogue sales and does not store its goods in the province generally does not have a permanent establishment in the province and, therefore, is not subject to apportionment.

Countries also apply the permanent establishment concept to determine whether a non-resident company has a sufficient connection with a jurisdiction for it to be drawn into that jurisdiction's tax system. In general, a country may subject a non-resident to income tax only if that non-resident has a permanent establishment in that country. A permanent establishment means a fixed place of business through which the business of an enterprise is wholly or partly carried on and includes, for example, a place of management, a branch, an office, a factory, etc.

If a permanent establishment exists, it may then be taxed, but only on the business profits attributable to a permanent establishment.[9] A non-resident company will not be deemed to have a permanent establishment merely because it has a subsidiary in a country, although in certain circumstances, the activities of the subsidiary may constitute a permanent establishment of the parent company.

The permanent establishment concept has a long history behind it. This concept arose in the Prussian industrial code of 1845 and was used in the 1899 income tax convention between Austria-Hungary and Prussia.[10] These early concepts of permanent establishment contain two main features that continue to exist today: the existence of a fixed place of business and a permanent nature of the business.

Although the permanent establishment concept has a long history behind it, it may not have a long future ahead of it, at least in its current form. The permanent establishment concept provided a sensible means to determine taxable presence when designed under 19th and early 20th century business conditions. Most companies did business in other countries through a physical presence, and it was easy to determine where that place of business was located. The main complication arose in determining whether the "fixed place of business" had existed long enough for it to have become a "permanent establishment."

In the 21st century, however, an increasing number of companies do business solely through an "intangible form" and do not require a physical presence to generate income. Their business in a location often does not have a permanent nature to it. It is notable that the list of examples of a permanent establishment does not include a reference to sales presence. Many of the new forms of remote businesses, however, earn substantial profits from their worldwide sales. In light of this evolution, it seems increasingly untenable to base jurisdiction to tax on a "fixed place of business" that has a "permanent" presence.

Other treaty-based substantial presence tests

Since at least 1981, the United States has required that all of its bilateral income treaties contain a provision limiting treaty benefits to those who are entitled to them. This provision is the limitation of benefits clause. The main purpose of this provision is to prevent so-called "treaty shopping" under which persons who are formally resident in a treaty jurisdiction do not have any real economic connection with the jurisdiction.

The EU may wish to consider applying the concepts under the limitations on benefits test to determine nexus. If a company has a sufficient connection to obtain tax treaty benefits from a country, then it seems logical to consider that it may also have a sufficient connection to be liable for paying taxes to that country.

5.2   THE TAX BASE

The European Commission's Common Consolidated Corporate Tax Base Working Group's first goal is to define the common EU-level tax base, and it is using financial information reported under the International Financial Reporting Standards as the starting point for measuring EU-level income.[11] One of the Working Group's main objectives is to determine the adjustments necessary to convert amounts prepared for financial purposes to amounts for purposes of the common tax base.[12]

Although the tax base definition is an important issue, this section does not attempt to duplicate the efforts already underway by the Working Group. Instead, it addresses some practical issues relating to how the U.S. states and Canadian provinces calculate their "common" tax bases and then how they modify their respective "common" tax bases to meet certain state and provincial objectives.

U.S. state taxable income

All U.S. corporations must file a Federal corporate income tax return (Form 1120). Nearly all of the U.S. states use U.S. federal taxable income from Form 1120 as the starting point for determining the state tax base.[13] A state may use taxable income before net operating losses and special deductions (line 28) or taxable income after net operating losses and special deductions (line 30). Nearly all states require taxpayers to include a complete copy or portions of the federal income tax return with the state income tax return. Although all of the states modify the tax base to some extent, they initially begin with the same definition of the total tax base.

The Federal tax return is also the source for many of the amounts used for calculating the apportionment factors. Along with providing information concerning gross income and deductions on Form 1120, corporations also must provide balance sheet information (assets, liabilities, and shareholders' equity) as part of the Federal tax return. Taxpayers must reconcile (on Schedule M-1) their book income with income reported for tax purposes.[14] The Federal tax return generally provides enough information for a taxpayer to calculate total taxable income and the totals for the apportionment factors.

The U.S. states do not simply use the Federal tax base as the pre-apportionment state tax base, however. All of the states offer various credits, depreciation rules, investment incentives, etc., and they do not automatically adopt the Federal definition of the taxable group. As no two state tax laws are identical, the outcome of this process is that a single federal tax base is transformed into 45 different tax bases. A taxpayer that had initially computed a common tax base for federal purposes no longer has a "common" tax base for state tax purposes.

This situation has an interesting parallel in the European Union. Apart from the fact that an EU taxpayer does not use a common EU-level tax base as a starting point, the situation in the EU Member States mirrors the situation in the U.S. states. All of the Member States offer their own tax credits, depreciation rules, investment incentives, etc., and have their own definition of the taxable group. Since no two Member State tax bases are identical, an EU multinational enterprise may face up to 25 different tax bases in the European Union.[15]

Business income and non-business income

States generally distinguish between business income and non-business income.[16] Business income is generally any income arising from transactions and activity in the regular course of the taxpayer's trade or business. Non-business income is any income that is not business income.

States apportion business income by formula and allocate non-business income to specific locations. In some cases, states allocate non-business income to the location of the physical property or where the intangible property (e.g., a patent) is used. In other cases, states allocate the items of income (e.g., interest and dividends) to the taxpayer's commercial domicile.[17]

EU Member States may wish to continue their current treatment of these specific categories of income.[18] The domestic laws of most countries categorize certain items of income, such as dividends, interest, royalties and other income, either as business profits or as investment income. The categorization affects the tax treatment of these items of income. Business profits of non-residents are taxed on a net basis, that is, after deducting expenses incurred to earn the business income. Amounts treated as investment income derived by non-residents are subject to a flat-rate withholding tax on a gross basis.[19]

The mechanics of the state corporate income tax

This next section takes a practical turn and illustrates how a taxpayer calculates its state corporate income tax liability.

Starting with the "common" measure of total U.S. income and (after adjusting for differences in the composition of the consolidated return, if needed), the taxpayer adds and subtracts certain items to obtain total net income, which includes both business and non-business income. Since business income is subject to apportionment while non-business income is subject to specific allocation, the taxpayer subtracts any net non-business income to obtain a measure of total business income.

Table 10 illustrates the typical calculations for state taxable income for a multistate corporation.

A taxpayer calculates its state business income by multiplying its total business income by the state's apportionment formula. It adds any non-business income allocated to the state to obtain total state income, which it multiplies by the state tax rate to obtain its tentative tax liability. The taxpayer then takes into account any state-specific tax credits to obtain its tax due.[20]

Table10. Computation of state taxable income for a multistate corporation

	Federal taxable income (before net operating losses)
+	Additions to Federal income
-	Subtractions from Federal income
=	Net income
-	Net non-business income allocated everywhere
=	Net business income subject to apportionment
x	State apportionment ratio
=	Net business income apportioned to the state
+	Net income allocated to the state
-	Net operating loss apportioned to the state (if necessary)
=	State taxable income
x	State tax rate
=	State tax liability before credits
-	State tax credits
=	State tax liability post credits

Source: Modified from Edmiston (2001) who drew from the *Official Code of Georgia* (OCGA) section 48-7-31; Department of Revenue, Income Tax Division, State of Georgia, Form 600. ¬

Provincial taxable income

The Canadian Federal government, through the Canada Revenue Agency (CRA), collects the federal and provincial tax for provinces that participate in the Federal Collection Agreements (FCAs). Under the FCAs, the Federal government agrees to incur the collection costs for the provincial corporate income tax in exchange for the provinces agreeing to use the federal tax base and formula.[21] The FCAs have been very successful. Only one province, Alberta, has left the agreements since they were created in 1962. In 2005, Ontario indicated its intention to rejoin the collection agreements, so that Alberta and Quebec (which has never participated in the agreements) would be the only two provinces that do not participate in the collection agreements.

The provincial tax base is derived from the Federal Corporation Income Tax Return, Form T2, which is the combined federal, provincial, and territorial tax return for the participating provinces. The ten provinces and three territories levy corporate income taxes.[22]

Taxpayers must include a complete financial statement for the tax year of the return using the General Index of Financial Information (GIFI). The federal tax base generally begins with information reported on the taxpayer's financial statements.[23] This amount is then adjusted to obtain a measure of total Canadian taxable income. Taxpayers include the GIFI with their tax return.

The Federal government apportions this income to the provinces using the payroll and gross receipts formula and then applies the provincial specific tax rate to calculate pre-credit provincial tax payable. It reduces this amount by any provincial-specific credits to obtain the final provincial tax payable. Provinces may set their own tax rates, levy surtaxes, and provide tax credits. Thus, the participating provinces determine their own corporate income tax policies, but the federal tax authority administers them.

Two of the provinces that do not participate in the FCAs also use the federal tax base as the starting point for calculating the tax base (Quebec does not). Alberta and Ontario both allow corporations to calculate taxable income differently from federal income. To help ensure compliance with the income apportionment, Alberta and Ontario require taxpayers to attach the federal schedule showing the apportionment factors across all of the provinces. Regardless of whether the province participates in the FCAs or not, however, taxpayers must report the factors in each province. Thus, the provincial governments ensure that the sum of the factor shares equals 100 percent.

The non-agreeing provinces follow federal definitions, in part, because they do not have the audit capability to verify the total tax base, and they rely on Federal audits to identify any adjustments to taxpayer income. Maintaining conformity of the provincial tax base with the federal tax base helps during these audits. The federal and provincial governments have also agreed to an exchange of information on taxpayer affairs.

Provincial tax authorities have typically not focused on inter-provincial transfer pricing issues, although this situation may be changing. For example, Ontario is considering undertaking detailed audits of transfer pricing arrangements between entities located in Ontario and their related entities in other provinces within Canada, and possibly in international jurisdictions.[24]

5.3   THE TAXABLE UNIT

The taxable unit and how its income is distributed across locations is an important part of the formulary apportionment system. The taxable unit can generally be defined as a single entity, as a consolidated corporate group, or as a unitary combined group. The taxable unit's income can then be allocated across locations using separate accounting principles or using a formula. This section discusses these issues, using illustrations from Canada, selected EU Member States, and the U.S. states.

The Canadian provinces' experience provides useful guidance in using a formula to distribute a common tax base across locations. The U.S. states' experience provides useful guidance for distributing a combined or consolidated tax base across locations.

Canada

The method of allocating income across the provinces depends on how the multiprovincial company has structured its operations.[25] Since Canada does not allow groups of affiliated corporations to consolidate their income for tax purposes, a company doing business in several provinces through separate subsidiaries in each province determines the income for each subsidiary corporation according to the separate accounts of each corporation. By contrast, a company doing business in more than one province through branches or sales offices (permanent establishments) uses a common formula to apportion its income across the provinces.[26]

Despite the lack of consolidation, the Canadian provinces appear to have experienced fewer problems than the U.S. states with cross-border income shifting and with entity restructuring.[27] This outcome may be due to the common provincial tax base, common apportionment formula, and common nexus standard for determining the taxable connection with the province. Although taxpayers would like some mechanism to obtain relief when one corporation in a corporate group has losses while others have profits, there are few pressures to move toward consolidation, primarily to avoid risking a break in the general uniformity of the Canadian tax base. By not allowing consolidation, the Canadian approach avoids the difficulties in defining the consolidated group.

All of the provinces levy a corporate income tax so that even though tax rates vary across the provinces, there are no tax-exempt provincial "tax havens." By contrast, there are "tax haven" states in the U.S. that do not tax corporate income or that provide tax-favored treatment of certain types of income.

Although the provinces use a common tax base and a common formula, the provincial corporate income tax system is far from uniform. Each province sets its own tax rates. All provinces provide tax credits, such as for film production, logging taxes, research and development. Using data for rates expected to be in place in 2008, Mintz (2004) shows that the effective corporate tax rates on capital for large corporations range from 17 percent in Newfoundland to 35 percent in Manitoba.

The rules for allocating income across locations within Canada contrast with those generally used at the international level where each branch (permanent establishment) that is part of a multinational enterprise is treated separately for purposes of determining the taxable profits of each branch (permanent establishment). The profits attributed to a permanent establishment are those that the permanent establishment would have made if it had been dealing with an entirely separate enterprise.[28]

The provincial experience provides very helpful guidance for implementing formulary apportionment of a common EU-level tax base. However, its experience does not provide guidance in using separate accounting with arm's length pricing as the "apportionment mechanism" for a common tax base.

Consolidation

The European Commission supports applying a common consolidated tax base to EU-level profits.[29] A consolidated group generally consists of the parent company and its affiliates that exceed a certain ownership threshold. That threshold is generally based on direct or indirect ownership of a percentage of shares based on vote or value. Members of the affiliated group eliminate intercompany transactions when calculating the consolidated tax base. Thus, transfer pricing is no longer necessary for tax purposes for transactions within the corporate group.

The consolidated group can be limited to the geographic borders of a country or a group of countries, or it may extend to worldwide operations.

Water's edge consolidation

The European Commission has proposed limiting the consolidated tax base to the territorial boundaries of the European Union. Water's edge consolidation is a means to limit the company tax system to entities and income within the territorial boundaries of the European Union. This approach essentially creates a company tax system limited to the European Union.

Under EU water's edge consolidation, EU multinationals use consolidated base taxation and formulary apportionment within the European Union. The traditional separate accounting and arm's length rules continue to apply for transactions outside of the European Union.[30]

Worldwide consolidation

Worldwide consolidation is the most expansive way to define the members of the taxable group. The group includes related corporations that meet the ownership threshold, regardless of where they are incorporated.

For guidance in this area, the EU may look to its own Member States. Denmark and Italy, for example, give taxpayers the option of filing either on a worldwide consolidated basis or on a domestic consolidated basis. The details of each country's system vary.[31]

Unitary combined reporting

Many U.S. states apply the concept of "unitary combined reporting," on a mandatory or elective basis, to determine the taxable group.[32] Under unitary combined reporting, the taxable unit generally includes a group of commonly controlled corporations and divisions engaged in integrated economic activity. The unitary business principle may apply to the activities of a single entity or to multiple legal entities.[33]

A unitary business is a business that has common control, common management, integrated operations, and, in general, a flow of value among the related entities. Members of the unitary business are combined and effectively treated as a single unitary business. The unitary group calculates its combined taxable income, net of intercompany transactions, and applies a combined formula to distribute income according to the location of the apportionment factors for the unitary group

The unitary method is a means to distribute the income of an integrated unitary business doing business across geographical boundaries.[34] The unitary method captures the notion that an economically integrated company has a value beyond the individual members of the company. A vertically integrated firm, for example, may have a different cost structure than a non-integrated firm. In this respect, the flow of value among the related parts of the unitary business may make the total income of a unitary business greater than the sum of the individual elements.[35] The fact that the unitary business may cross geographic or legal borders does not alter this relationship.

The unitary business notion also helps prevent tax shifting through manipulation of the corporate form. In part, California expanded the unitary combined report procedure in the 1930s to protect the state tax base against practices in the motion picture industry of producing a film in one corporation and transferring the film to an out-of-state distribution corporation. By creating a legally separate out-of-state subsidiary, the integrated company isolated its expenses in one corporation and its revenue in another corporation and shifted its income out of the state. Since the out-of-state subsidiary had no taxable connection with California, the state could not include it in the state taxable group. Under the unitary business method, however, the tax authority may look beyond the legal fiction of the corporate group to examine the actual economic relationships within the corporate group.[36] If those relationships reflect a unitary business, then the state may combine the operations into a single unitary business report and distribute the combined income across locations using formulary apportionment.

The unitary business method has advantages. One advantage is that it examines the substance rather than the form of the relationship among various entities. It treats the related members of an integrated firm as a single entity, not as a collection of unrelated entities. In cases where the activities of related enterprises are so interrelated that the group effectively makes up a single enterprise, the unitary business method treats that enterprise as a single unit for tax purposes.

The unitary business method also has disadvantages. A key disadvantage is that there is no "bright line" definition of a unitary business.[37] A unitary business has an "exchange of value" among the commonly-controlled elements of a unitary business. It may have functional integration, centralized management, and economies of scale; it may have unity of ownership, unity of operation, and unity of use; it may have operational interdependence; and it may have economic interdependence.[38] Determining the contours of a unitary business in the U.S. states has become a fact-intensive and often contentious process.[39]

Many U.S. state courts as well as the U.S. Supreme Court have been called upon to determine whether a taxpayer constitutes a unitary business with its related members. In each case, the decision required an in-depth analysis of the facts and circumstances. The underlying concept of the unitary business suggests that it may not be possible to provide a single definition of a unitary business.

The U.S. Supreme Court appears to have given the last word on this matter. As the Court noted, "A final point that needs to be made about the unitary business concept is that it is not, so to speak unitary: there are variations on the theme, and any number of them are logically consistent with the underlying principle motivating the approach."[40]

Notes

1. States are subject to limitations imposed under Federal law (Public Law 86-272) that establish that a state (or local) government may not impose a net income tax on an out-of-state seller if the seller's only connection with a state is to solicit orders for sales of tangible personal property that are delivered from outside the state.

2. See Shay, Fleming, and Peroni (2002) who assert that the country that provides a market has a legitimate claim to tax the income from sales and services in that country. See Musgrave (1984, 2000) for similar arguments in the U.S. state and European Union context. Tax treaty negotiators have traditionally rejected the approach of imposing an income tax solely on the presence of sales, and business groups have resisted becoming subject to income tax in a jurisdiction merely because they have sales in that jurisdiction. For an evaluation of these issues in the context of new business methods, see OECD (2003a).

3. In a case dealing with a remote vendor's obligation to collect use taxes due on sales to in-state purchasers, the U.S. Supreme Court ruled that the vendor must have a physical presence in the state to create the required "substantial nexus" necessary to satisfy Commerce Clause requirements. See *Quill Corp. v. North Dakota*, 504 U.S. 298, 112 S. Ct. 1904, 119 L. Ed. 2d 91 (1992). Quill involved attempts by a state to require out-of-state mail-order vendors to collect and remit use taxes on goods purchased by in-state customers even though the vendors had no outlets or sales representatives in the state.

4. Delaware exempts income of a Delaware holding company from state corporate income tax. See 30 Del. C. section 1902(b)(8).

5. *Geoffrey Inc. v. South Carolina Tax Commission*, 437 S.E. 2d 13, cert. denied, 114 S. Ct. 550 (1993). See Jerome Hellerstein (1995) for an analysis of Geoffrey and the nexus requirements for the state corporate income tax.

6. *Lanco, Inc. v. Director, Division of Taxation*, 21 N.J. Tax 200 (2003). Lanco has no offices, employees, or real or tangible property in New Jersey. Lanco licenses Lane Bryant, Inc., to utilize the intangible property in the conduct of Lane Bryant's retail operations, including those

in New Jersey, and in return receives royalty payments from Lane Bryant. Lanco and Lane Bryant are affiliated corporations.

7. See *Lanco, Inc. v. Director, Division of Taxation*, _____ N.J. Super. ___, ___ A2d ___ (App. Div. 2005). I am grateful to Walter Hellerstein for alerting me to this decision.

8. See Regulation 400(2) for examples of fixed places of businesses and see Income Tax Interpretation Bulletin IT-177R2 (Consolidated) from the Canada Revenue Agency and subsection 400(2) of the Regulations. The definition is similar but not identical to the treaty definition. See the Income Tax Act, RSC 1985, c. 1 (5th Supp.), as amended, regulation 400(2).

9. In determining the amount of business profits attributable to the permanent establishment, the permanent establishment is treated as a functionally separate taxpayer and the arm's length principle applies. See Article 5 (Permanent Establishment) and the related Commentary of the OECD Model Tax Convention (2005).

10. For further history, see Resch (2003). In his view, Prussia's interest in developing this idea related to its political aims to create an economically unified Germany and to remove obstacles between the German states that impeded trade and investment. The smaller states initially resisted this notion, apparently over fears of revenue losses.

11. Since January 1, 2005, publicly-traded companies in the European Union have been required to use International Financial Reporting Standards. See CCCTB\WP\001 10 December 2004, and CCCTB\WP\005 21 January 2005. The rules under IFRS may have large effects on the EU company financial accounts. As an example, Unilever shows that its net profit in 2004 rises to €2,755 million under IFRS from €1,876 million reported in its consolidated profit and loss account. By contrast, the difference in Unilever's profits IFRS and under U.S. GAAP (€2,686 million) is narrower. The U.S. Securities and Exchange Commission requires listed companies to prepare their accounts under U.S. standards. By contrast, Canada allows foreign companies cross-listed in Canada to use IFRS without reconciling them to Canadian standards.

12. See Manzon and Plesko (2002) for a detailed explanation of the relation between financial and tax reporting measures of income.

13. Foreign corporations file their Federal tax returns on Form 1120-F. As an interesting historical point, the U.S. Federal government modeled its corporate income tax on the state corporate income tax. In 1911, Wisconsin became the first state to adopt a corporate income tax, and this state law became a model for the federal government when it adopted the corporate income tax two years later. Thomas S. Adams, a professor of economics and later a Wisconsin Tax Commissioner, helped design the Wisconsin law. Following his work in Wisconsin, Adams worked for the U.S. Treasury Department, where he was a delegate to the League of Nations committee that helped design the international tax rules. See Graetz and O'Hear (1997) for a discussion of the role Adams played in shaping U.S. state, U.S. Federal and international tax policy. Hellerstein and Hellerstein (2005) call the Wisconsin tax the "father of twentieth-century corporate income taxation."

14. See Plesko (2002) for a reconciliation of U.S. book and tax data based on information provided in Schedule M-1 of the U.S. Federal corporate income tax return.

15. To some extent, the taxpayer may have a common total tax base under IFRS. This amount, however, is generally not limited to income and operations located in the European Union and it is financial, not tax, income. The difference between financial and tax income may be reconciled following a procedure such as that described for the U.S. in Manzon and Plesko (2002).

16. Hellerstein and McLure (2004) explain that "[A] state may not tax even an apportioned share of the taxpayer's income tax base with which it has no constitutionally cognizable connection."

17. For an evaluation of some issues concerning state treatment of non-business income, see Walter Hellerstein (1993).

18. Arnold (2003) notes that the "distinction between business and investment income is a fundamental part of the structure of existing tax treaties" and that, even though the distinction is

"problematic at the margins," the distinction between these types of income will continue to be a feature of tax treaties and the domestic laws in most countries.

19. For details, see Articles 7 (Business Profits), 10 (Dividends), 11 (Interest), 12 (Royalties), and 21 (Other Income) of the OECD Model Tax Convention (2005).

20. In defining the EU tax base, the Commission may wish to consider allowing the EU Member States to offer such credits, provided the credits meet EU rules on state aid. As shown in chapter 7, the Canadian provinces provide such credits and, therefore, retain significant policy flexibility.

21. All references to provinces also include the territories. I am grateful to Robert Brown for helpful assistance on this subject.

22. See Treff and Perry (2003) for additional details about the provincial corporate tax systems.

23. See Guide to the General Index of Financial Information (GIFI) for Corporations, RC4088(E), Rev. 05, Canada Revenue Agency.

24. See Przysuski and Lalapet (2005) for a discussion of the Ontario proposal. The motivation for the change arises from two concerns. First, Ontario has a relatively high corporate income tax rate, so there is an incentive to shift profits out of Ontario. Second, since Ontario is the largest and wealthiest province, many multinational and multiprovincial corporations operate there. Thus, there are many opportunities for companies to shift losses to their Ontario branches and permanent establishments

25. This section draws from the description of provincial corporate income taxation in Mintz and Smart (2004).

26. A non-resident company must have a permanent establishment in the province before it can be subject to tax on its profits. The definition of permanent establishment at the provincial level differs slightly from the definition at the federal level. However, if under the provisions of a tax treaty, a non-resident does not have a Canadian permanent establishment, then it also will not have a permanent establishment for provincial purposes.

27. However, see the analysis by Mintz and Smart (2004) in chapter 7 for a discussion of income shifting in the provinces.

28. See Article 7 (Business Profits) of the OECD Model Tax Convention and OECD (2003a) for an explanation of these approaches. See OECD (2004a) for a discussion of proposed modifications to the rules for attributing profits to permanent establishments.

29. Recall that the subtitle of its Communication (Commission, 2001) refers to a strategy for providing companies with a consolidated corporate tax base for their EU-wide activities.

30. McDaniel (1994) analyzes issues involved under formulary apportionment in the three NAFTA countries. As he explains, limiting the scope of the unitary business to a sub-group of countries implies that "all of the rules ... that are barriers to cross-border trade and investment would continue with respect to trade and investment outside NAFTA. Source rules would be needed, and arm's length pricing would continue to be used for non-NAFTA related companies." McDaniel suggests, however, that this requirement may have the effect of encouraging companies to invest in the NAFTA countries.

31. This pattern suggests a predictable outcome --- 25 different definitions of the worldwide consolidated group in the European Union.

32. A full analysis of these issues is beyond the scope of this text. See Hellerstein and Hellerstein (1998, cum. Supp. 2005) for a detailed evaluation of unitary combined reporting. See McDaniel (1994) for an analysis of issues concerning a system of "formulary taxation of the unitary enterprise" within the NAFTA water's edge.

33. The U.S. Supreme Court sanctioned the use of the unitary business principle in 1920 in a case concerning a U.K. company doing business in the United States through branches. See *Bass, Ratcliff & Gretton v. State Tax Commission*, 266 U.S. 271 (1920).

34. The same logic that applies the unitary business principle to a head office and branches also applies to a parent company and its subsidiaries. See Keesling and Warren (1960) for a dis-

cussion of the development of the unitary report in California. Frank Keesling is considered the "father" of the unitary combined reporting concept.

35. The first significant ruling in California concerning the unitary business occurred in 1941 in *Butler Bros. v. McColgan*, 17 Cal. 2d. 664 (1941). The California Court rejected the company's request to use separate accounting, noting that such a method may only properly be used when income may be segregated clearly and accurately, an effort that the Court found can not be done in the case of integrated interstate operations.

36. The California Court sanctioned the application of the unitary business notion to a corporation with multiple entities in *Edison California Stores v. McColgan*, 30 Cal. 2d 472 (1947). As Keesling and Warren (1960) explain, "the principles governing the allocation of income of a unitary business were the same whether that business is conducted by one corporation with several divisions, as in the Butler Bros. case, or by several corporations with common ownership and control, as in the Edison case."

37. A bright-line test does not eliminate this issue. See, for example, *Kroger Co. v. Fisher*, No. 02 CV 6564 in Colorado where the parties litigated over whether the taxpayer met the bright-line tests.

38. At first glance, it may seem that the states should use federal consolidation rules as the sole basis for determining whether a business is unitary, on the assumption, perhaps, that this degree of ownership presumes a unitary business. It is not clear, however, that this idea would "pass Constitutional muster" if applied on a mandatory basis. Under the unitary business idea, a non-resident creates a taxable connection through being part of a unitary business. In such a case, the state may subject its income to apportionment through the unitary combination process. Ownership alone does not create that connection.

39. Colorado has established a series of tests for evaluating whether a unitary business exists. For example, if common ownership exists, then a company will be unitary with another if it meets three of six specific tests relating to shares of intercompany sales, number of business services, etc. See 39-22-303(11)(a) C.R.S.

40. See *Container Corp. v. Franchise Tax Board*, 463, U.S. 159 (1983). As with the definition of the apportionment formula, there is no single correct unitary business definition. What is most important is to agree on a definition and then remain with that definition.

Chapter 6

TAX ADMINISTRATION, COMPLIANCE AND TAX PLANNING

No tax system can operate without a tax administration. However, that does not mean that the EU must create a new supra-national fiscal authority, or that the EU must wait for the creation of an international tax organization before proceeding with its comprehensive company tax reform. The European Union does not have an EU tax authority, nor is the EU likely to create such an authority in the near future.

Under current political structures, implementing an EU-level tax base with formulary apportionment must rely on the tax authorities in the individual Member States and on any "multistate" organizations that the EU Member States may develop, as discussed below. If the Member State where the company is resident is responsible for auditing the total tax base, then a reasonable amount of cooperation among EU tax authorities coupled with guidance from EU businesses may be sufficient to implement and administer the proposed company tax system.

The U.S. states provide some examples of the type of organizations that the European Union may consider creating to help administer a formulary apportionment system. An important feature of the U.S. state organizations, in particular, is that the states voluntarily formed these organizations.

This chapter addresses issues that arise when a tax system crosses jurisdictional borders: administration, compliance, tax planning and how governments respond to multistate corporate tax planning. Much of the discussion is designed to provide the European Union a glimpse into how the U.S. states and Canadian provinces administer their formulary apportionment systems.

6.1   MULTISTATE TAX ORGANIZATIONS IN THE UNITED STATES

Since the states use Federal income as the starting point for measuring the total tax base, they generally rely on the federal government to verify the total U.S. tax base.[1] The Internal Revenue Service (IRS) is responsible for auditing the total tax base and verifying that taxpayers have properly reported their U.S. income. The IRS may provide federal tax return information to state tax agencies as long as that information is used only for tax administration purposes and is protected against improper disclosure or release.

The IRS does not address issues concerning a shift of income from one U.S. state to another since those shifts generally do not affect the taxpayer's federal tax liability. State tax authorities tend to focus on issues concerning apportionment and the composition of the taxable group. In this process, they may work with various multistate organizations.

Multistate tax organizations

State tax authorities and multistate businesses cooperate through many organizations, including the Multistate Tax Commission (MTC), the Federation of Tax Administrators (FTA), and the Council on State Taxation (COST). Through these groups, state tax authorities and multistate businesses work together to attempt to resolve problems that arise in the multistate context.

In the late 1960s, the states developed a model state tax statute, the Multistate Tax Compact, which adopts the provisions of the Uniform Division of Income for Tax Purposes Act.[2] Some states have incorporated the provisions of UDITPA verbatim in their tax codes.[3]

The Multistate Tax Commission, which is comprised of the principal state tax administrators, is an important group working in the multistate tax area.[4] In addition to developing the allocation and apportionment regulations discussed earlier, the MTC operates several programs designed to improve compliance with multistate corporate income tax requirements. For example, the MTC runs a voluntary joint audit program that allows tax authorities to verify the apportionment percentages and amounts of income allocated to several states.

The Federation of Tax Administrators, which is an organization of state government tax administrators, works to enhance compliance with the state corporate income tax system. For example, the FTA has developed a Uniform Exchange of Information Agreement through which states routinely share confidential data. Each state's statute indicates how this data will be used, including how confidential data will be destroyed.

The FTA also regularly meets with federal tax authorities to discuss and coordinate their activities. For example, the U.S. Department of the Treasury and the IRS announced in September 2003 a "new partnership" with state tax administrators to combat abusive tax avoidance transactions.[5] Under this program, the IRS, cities and states exchange information to prevent abusive tax avoidance transactions and share resources to address common compliance concerns.

The states often cooperate with one another to verify the apportionment factors and the share of income apportioned across the states. For example, the MTC and the FTA have formed a joint task force to work on improving the amount of interstate information sharing that takes place among the states.

Multistate companies are also involved in the process of shaping multistate tax practices. Much of this activity occurs through the Council on State Taxation, a trade association composed of multistate corporations involved in interstate and international business.

COST representatives frequently work with state tax authorities and multistate agencies, such as the FTA and MTC. For example, COST and the FTA formed an electronic data interchange task force that produced the Model Recordkeeping and Retention Regulation. COST and the MTC jointly developed the Multistate Tax Commission Multistate Alternative Dispute Resolution Procedure that provides taxpayers an optional forum to resolve multistate tax controversies. COST also participates in the MTC's public policy working groups to assist in drafting uniform multistate tax regulations, including developing uniform definitions for business and non-business income and for a unitary business.

Since the states and businesses voluntarily established these organizations, their experiences may provide particularly helpful guidance to the EU Member States and to EU businesses. To some extent, UNICE may fulfill a role similar to the Council on State Taxation. The European Commission may also consider creating organizations similar to the Joint Transfer Pricing Forum and the Common Consolidated Tax Base Working Group to perform functions similar to those described above.[6]

6.2   COMPLIANCE COSTS

One of the Commission's main goals is to reduce the compliance costs that arise from the interaction of the different Member State company tax systems in the European Union. Companies doing business in more than one EU Member State have higher compliance costs than those doing business only locally.[7] As long as jurisdictions apply different tax rules, compliance will inevitably rise when companies expand across borders. The issue, therefore, is when do compliance costs create a tax obstacle to cross-border investment.

There are many explanations for high compliance costs. Some arise because the tax system, itself, is complex. To gain an appreciation of one type of compliance cost, consider the estimated costs to comply with certain income tax information returns required under U.S. Federal law. These costs include time spent on record keeping, learning about the law or the form, and preparing and sending the form to the tax authority.[8] For example, the IRS estimates that taxpayers will spend 142 hours complying with the information requirements for a controlled foreign corporation.[9]

Companies also voluntarily incur many compliance costs as part of their overall business strategy. Thus, compliance costs are not always 'obstacles' to cross-border investment. For example, a company will voluntarily incur certain tax planning costs if the benefits from the tax planning activity outweigh its compliance costs. To prevent abuse, many tax authorities require additional documentation when a taxpayer earns income in a tax-favored form, which increases compliance costs.

Mills, Erickson, and Maydew (1998) describe the difference between tax compliance costs and tax planning costs as follows: "Consider a firm that sets up a special tax entity . . . for tax-planning purposes. Most would consider the costs associated with deciding to form this entity and the costs of setting up the entity to be tax planning. However, this special entity will also require additional tax-related expenditures as long as it remains in existence. Reasonable differences of opinion exist as to whether these ongoing costs are more correctly labeled 'tax planning' or 'tax compliance'."

Taxpayers and tax authorities are likely to agree on the importance of reducing compliance costs. Providing fewer opportunities for tax-motivated transactions would simplify the tax rules, and, therefore, reduce complexity. However, it is not clear that taxpayers would welcome the outcome if it increases their tax payments. Moreover, although simplification is desirable for many reasons, it also imposes costs on revenue, equity, efficiency, and compliance. Some tax code complexity is necessary to achieve these other goals.[10]

6.3 TAX PLANNING

As suggested above, restricting tax base shifting is an important objective for EU tax policy makers. Many U.S. states have become aware of new tax planning opportunities and are considering various ways to respond.

Therefore, in designing an EU apportionment formula, the Member States should consider whether the chosen formula adequately protects against inappropriate income shifting. As discussed in chapter 4, certain design principles guide the choice of apportionment factors. A formula that distributes income according to mobile firm-specific factors creates profit-shifting opportunities. As long as it can change the location of the factors used to apportion income, a firm may shift its income to tax-favored locations. Since state and provincial corporate tax rates are not uniform, multistate and multiprovincial firms have an incentive to shift their factors to low tax states or provinces.

Multistate firms have additional tax planning opportunities that do not arise in Canada. Unlike the Canadian provinces, the U.S. states have different nexus standards, different apportionment formulae, different business and non-business income definitions, and different group definitions.

In recent years, many U.S. state tax analysts have noted that the state corporate income tax makes up an increasingly smaller share of income. Fox and Luna (2002) provide four main explanations for the shrinking tax base: cyclical reductions in corporate profits, declines in the federal corporate tax base, state policy changes, and "more aggressive corporate tax planning." State corporate tax revenues will generally fall if corporate profits are cyclically low, just as they may fall if the state reduces its corporate income tax rate. Neither of these declines is due to inappropriate state tax planning. However, declines due to creating entities in tax-favored locations may be a result of aggressive tax planning.

Factor shifting

This section briefly discusses the issue of factor shifting. With apportionment, a company cannot generally shift income through transfer pricing, but it can shift income by re-locating its factors. Since the company controls the location of each of these factors to some extent (i.e., the factors are endogenous), the factors are susceptible to being "re-located" for tax minimization purposes.

Factor-shifting opportunities arise in the U.S. states because the states apply different factor definitions. However, even if factor definitions are identical, as in the Canadian provinces, income-shifting opportunities still exist as long as tax rates differ across locations. Under apportionment, a company has an incentive to locate its apportionment factors in low-tax locations.

The components of the apportionment factors shown earlier in table 8 suggest elements of the apportionment factor that the firm may be able to re-locate. For example, the sales (gross receipts) factor is viewed as a highly mobile factor. This mobility may be due to how the state or province records the sale. Firms may alter the location of a sale by altering the location where it is delivered or where the title is transferred. This technique can be particularly important if the taxpayer is located in a state that does not return sales made in a location where they are not taxed back to the state of origin (i.e., the state does not apply the throwback rule).

Since altering the property factor may require moving the physical location of property, it is less mobile than the sales factor. For example, a taxpayer cannot readily move land and buildings. However, since the property factor includes inventory, a company may re-locate the property factor to some extent by storing inventory or locating distribution centers in a low-tax area. If the property factor includes intangible property, then the property factor becomes more mobile than it is now since intangible property, by definition, does not have a fixed location.

The payroll factor is generally considered the factor least susceptible to manipulation, in large part because the location of payroll is derived from federal definitions of payroll. Nevertheless, multistate companies may shift the location of their payroll for tax reasons. For example, since the payroll factor generally includes only payments made to employees, a company may reduce the payroll factor by hiring independent contractors. If the payroll factor does not include fringe benefits, providing compensation in the form of such benefits rather than as wages can reduce payroll. If payroll includes executive compensation, then companies may choose to move their headquarters to low tax areas to shift payroll to these areas.

Passive Investment Companies

In recent years, a growing number of multistate companies have formed intangible property holding companies, or passive investment companies (PICs), as part of their overall state tax planning strategy. This strategy is particularly valuable for companies doing business in states that do not require combination.

Under this tax planning strategy, an operating company doing business in a separate-entity state sets up a holding company in a state that treats investment income favorably and then transfers its intangible property to that holding company. The holding company licenses the intangible property back to the operating company, which pays it royalties for the right to use the intangible property. The operating company then claims a tax deduction for the royalty payment as a legitimate business expense. The operating company reduces its tax payments, and the holding company pays little or no tax on the royalty income to its home state. Furthermore, if the holding company does not have a taxable presence outside of its home state, it may be able to avoid paying any state tax on this income.[11]

An intangible holding company can provide other tax benefits. In addition to licensing its intellectual property in exchange for royalty payments, the holding company may subsequently loan any excess operating funds back to the related operating companies. The holding company receives interest income for these loans, while the related company receives a tax deduction for the interest expense.

In most cases, the holding company will not have any offices, employees, tangible property, or other physical connection with the taxing state. By not "doing business" in the state, i.e., the holding company does not create a taxable presence in the state, the holding company avoids being drawn into that state's tax system. If the taxing state does not require consolidation or a combined report, then the in-state taxpayer will not include the out-of-state holding company in its state tax calculation.

6.4   GOVERNMENTAL RESPONSES

As the states have become aware of these income shifting opportunities, they have attempted to implement legislative measures to reduce or limit the revenue loss from these strategies. States generally pursue one of two legislative techniques. Mandatory combined reporting is the most comprehensive solution. A more common solution, however, is to disallow deductions for certain intercompany expenses or to add back such expenses to the tax base. States also act through the judicial process, but this process can be time-consuming and create uncertainty.[12]

Mandatory combined reporting restricts many tax-planning opportunities created through the use of intangible holding companies or passive investment companies. Combining the income and apportionment factors of related entities in a single report eliminates intercompany transactions so that when a company files a combined report, the holding company's intangible income offsets the operating company's tax deductible payments. Thus, combined reporting can prevent companies from reducing taxable income by shifting passive investments to separately incorporated out-of-state holding companies and then making tax-deductible payments to these related entities.

Given its benefits in protecting the state tax base, a number of states have considered moving to the combined reporting system, including Arkansas, Connecticut, Iowa, Maryland, Massachusetts, Missouri, and Wisconsin, but only one state has adopted combined reporting in the past two decades.[13]

In 2004, Vermont adopted a unitary combined reporting system for affiliated entities effective in 2006. To make the legislative change revenue neutral, Vermont moved from the three-factor equally-weighted formula to a double-weighted sales formula and reduced its maximum statutory tax rate to 8.9 percent from 9.75 percent. According to a legislative analysis of the bill, the state adopted mandatory combined reporting to "put all corporations doing business in Vermont on an equal income tax footing" and to prevent companies from avoiding Vermont tax through the use of subsidiaries.[14]

Since businesses generally oppose state attempts to move to mandatory combined reporting, states often pursue other methods to restrict tax planning. One common method is to deny income tax deductions for certain intercompany expenses. In 1991, Ohio became the first state to implement statutory measures to combat against passive investment corporations.[15] Ohio generally disallows certain intercompany expense deductions and requires corporate taxpayers to add back certain interest, royalty, and other intangible expenses paid directly or indirectly to specified related persons. These provisions apply to payments made by "any related members whose activities, in any one state, are primarily limited to the maintenance and management of intangible investments."[16] The add-back provisions are directed towards related corporations in states that do

Table 11. Selected state policies

Policy	State
Mandatory combined reporting	Alaska, Arizona, California, Colorado, Hawaii, Idaho, Illinois, Kansas, Maine, Minnesota, Montana, Nebraska, New Hampshire, North Dakota, Oregon, Utah, Vermont (as of 2006)
Passive Investment Company legislation (year adopted)	Arkansas (2003), Alabama (2001), Connecticut (1998), Georgia (2005), Kentucky (2005) Maryland (2004), Massachusetts (2003), Mississippi (2001), New Jersey (2002), New York (2003), North Carolina (2001), Ohio (1991), Virginia (2004).
Mandatory separate entity filing	Delaware, Maryland, Pennsylvania, Texas, Wisconsin

Source: Shipley, Smith and Bauer (2004), Dennehy and Ehrlich (2004), and Healy (2001).

not tax the income; thus, to the extent that the income is taxed, the add-back provisions do not apply.

The trend to adopt anti-PIC measures is accelerating. As of 2005, thirteen states have adopted such measures, and another half dozen states were considering or had recently considered such legislation. The measures vary widely across the states. Many states, for example, provide exceptions to the "add-back measures" that will allow the tax deduction if the payment has a legitimate business purposes. Similarly, states may allow the tax deduction if the taxpayer can demonstrate that the out-of-state entity is engaged in substantial business activity. Finally, many states also respect the payment if the taxpayer demonstrates that the transaction occurred under arm's length terms. A review by Guariglia, Shipley, and Banks (2005) finds that the state provisions are unique.

Table 11 lists the states that have mandatory combined reporting, the states that have adopted related party expense disallowance measures (including the year the state adopted the measures), and the states that require separate-entity filing.

6.5   TAX PLANNING AND WATER'S EDGE REPORTING

To limit the tax system to the European Union's borders, the system must define what constitutes an EU company and its EU income. These rules are particularly important to prevent improper income shifting outside of the European Union. If the consolidated group does not cover worldwide operations but, instead, is limited to a certain geographic area, companies may have an incentive to shift income into or out of the EU for tax purposes.

To illustrate this situation, assume the EU adopts formulary apportionment with water's edge consolidation. Now, suppose an Italian company sets up a subsidiary in a non-EU tax haven that lends funds to its French subsidiary in exchange for interest payments. The French subsidiary deducts the interest payments, but the Italian parent company does not include the interest income as EU income because the tax haven entity receiving the payments is outside the EU's water's edge. Thus, the Italian company obtains a double benefit --- it gains a tax deduction for the interest payment and it is exempt from tax on the interest income.

EU Member States may wish to adopt measures to address the income shifting and tax haven concerns that may arise when the consolidated group has geographical limits such as the EU water's edge. These methods are not new to the European Union, as the international community already uses many of these techniques in its efforts to prevent improper income shifting.[17]

One way to address the income shifting concern is to include the tax haven within the water's edge. This outcome may be achieved by, for example, treating foreign subsidiaries located in tax haven countries as "EU corporations" and thus includible in the EU water's edge group. Income and expenses are eliminated as intracompany transactions and have no effect on the overall position so that the incentive to shift income is reduced.

Some U.S. states have adopted this approach. For example, since 2004, Montana includes in the water's edge group subsidiaries incorporated in certain listed tax havens.[18] An advantage of following this approach is that it piggybacks on the efforts underway in the EU and the OECD to curb the use of tax havens. Including tax haven entities within the water's edge assists these efforts. The EU Member States may also refer to the OECD's list of certain non-cooperative tax havens for purposes of determining the entities that it may consider including within the EU water's edge group.[19]

Instead of applying a list, the water's edge group may include a tax haven on the basis of how its tax rate compares to a base tax rate. For example, according to the EU Code of Conduct on Business Taxation, a measure is potentially harmful if it provides a significantly lower effective level of taxation compared with measures that generally apply, among others.

The EU Member States may employ other measures to restrict tax avoidance. For example, they may deny deductions for certain expenses related to generating exempt income in certain locations. Some EU countries take this route. Italy, for example, denies tax deductions for costs and expenses related to transactions with an enterprise resident in a non-EU Member State or territory if that territory offers a preferential regime. This response parallels the "anti-PIC" measures discussed above.

This action is also consistent with the OECD's efforts to curb harmful tax competition. The OECD (1998) recommends for future study the possibility of restricting deductions for payments to tax haven entities as a way of curbing harmful tax competition. A number of OECD member countries restrict tax deductions for payments made to tax havens or reverse the burden of proof for this type of payments. Spain, for example, denies tax deductions for services provided in tax havens unless an effective transaction has taken place.

The EU may take traditional approaches and reallocate income in cases where the tax haven corporation lacks a business purpose or is a "sham" corporation. Finally, the EU may restrict the improper use of tax havens by increasing the withholding tax rate on payments made to tax haven operations.

Notes

1. Apart from a few large states like California and New York, most state tax authorities do not have the resources necessary to conduct such audits. California's Revenue and Taxation Code grants the Franchise Tax Board the basic authority to reallocate income available to the IRS under Section 482. Section 25114 of the California tax code encompasses the language of Section 482 and was enacted with the water's edge provisions. For a discussion of California's experience in conducting formulary apportionment audits of multinational corporations, see U.S. GAO (1995).

2. The National Conference of Commissioners developed UDITPA in 1957. See Uniform Division of Income for Tax Purposes Act, 7A, Uniform Laws Annotated 331 (West 1985).

3. For example, section 25139 of the California Revenue and Tax Code indicates that Sections 25120 to 25139, inclusive, may be cited as the Uniform Division of Income for Tax Purposes Act.

4. For details, see www.mtc.gov. The MTC has an executive board whose members are generally not state tax authorities. MTC membership is voluntary.

5. See U.S. Department of the Treasury Office of Public Affairs press release JS-735, September 16, 2003. Details of the agreement are available in the Abusive Tax Avoidance Transaction (ATAT) Memorandum of Understanding, which is available on the IRS website. The agreement focuses on smaller corporations and wealthy individuals.

6. For details on these groups, see the relevant pages on the website: http://europa.eu.int/comm/taxation_customa/taxation/index.htm

7. See Commission (2004d), IP/04/1091. The Survey was based on a questionnaire concerning company taxation and VAT compliance costs in the EU sent via the European Business Test Panel to more than 2,000 companies. The Commission received responses from 700 companies in 14 Member States.

8. The IRS used results from a study commissioned to estimate compliance burdens for each tax form. The study estimated the compliance burden as a function of the number of line items on the form, the references to the Internal Revenue Code and regulations, and the number of attachments requested. For details, see Nelson (1999).

9. These estimates relate to preparing the information return (form 5471) that a U.S. company files for each of its controlled foreign corporations and not to the tax return (Form 1120).

10. For a discussion in the U.S. context, see Nelson (1999).

11. Since many of these transactions occur in Delaware because of the state's favorable incorporation laws and tax exemption of passive income, this situation is referred to as the "Delaware Passive Investment Corporation (PIC) Loophole." Recall that in the *Geoffrey* case discussed in chapter 5 that the company had $55 million in income but paid no income taxes to any state that year. Nevada is also a common holding company location since it does not tax corporate income. Also recall from chapter 5, that it was the creation of a subsidiary in Nevada by a California company that pushed California to expand its concept of the unitary business.

12. See Shipley, Smith, and Bauer (2004) for a review of key state cases in these areas. See Lippman (1998) for an early analysis of state challenges to related party transactions. Recall also the reversal in New Jersey in the *Lanco* decision discussed in chapter 5.

13. See Dagostino (2004).

14. See the statement of intent to H. 784 and No. 152 An Act Relating to Income Tax.

15. See Ohio Rev. Code section 5733.042(l)(12).

16. See Ohio Rev. Code section 5733.042(C)(1).

17. See, for example, the discussion in the U.S. Treasury Department report on deferral (2000). Exempting foreign income (or applying a different tax regime to foreign income) increases the importance of correctly allocating income and expenses between foreign and domestic sources.

18. See Montana Code Annotated 15-31-322 Water's Edge election --- inclusion of tax havens. These tax havens include Andorra, Anguilla, Antigua and Barbuda, Aruba, the Bahamas, Bahrain, Barbados, Belize, Bermuda, the British Virgin Islands, Cayman Islands, Cook Islands, Turks and Caicos Islands, Dominica, Gibraltar, Grenada, Guernsey-Sark-Alderney, Isle of Man, Jersey, Liberia, Liechtenstein, Luxembourg, Maldives, Marshall Islands, Monaco, Montserrat, Nauru, Netherlands Antilles, Nieu, Panama, Samoa, Seychelles, St. Kitts and Nevis, St. Lucia, St. Vincent and the Grenadines, Tonga, U.S. Virgin Islands, and Vanuatu.

19. See OECD (2000). The 2000 Report lists 35 jurisdictions that met the tax haven criteria listed in the 1998 Report. The OECD list is the same as the Montana list except that the OECD list does not include the Cayman Islands, Liechtenstein, and Luxembourg.

Chapter 7

ECONOMIC ANALYSIS OF FORMULARY APPORTIONMENT

This chapter examines some economic consequences that may arise under formulary apportionment. The chapter first provides a technical analysis and calculates potential "apportionment" tax rates for the EU Member States. It then reviews the empirical evidence from the U.S. states and Canadian provinces on how apportionment affects investment, employment, and sales decisions and how different formulae may affect tax revenues. A final section evaluates recent theoretical evidence on how formulary apportionment may affect tax competition in the European Union.

7.1 TECHNICAL ANALYSIS

McLure (1980, 1981) introduced the economic insight into how formulary apportionment may affect sub-national investment, employment, and sales decisions. Since the formula distributes income across states according to the location of property, payroll, and sales, the incidence effects that arise under apportionment are similar to the incidence effects of excise taxes levied directly on property, payroll, and sales in the state. Capital and labor bear the burden of the property and payroll elements; consumers bear the burden of the sales element. Unlike excise taxes, however, the factor taxes under apportionment are firm-specific. Thus, they may introduce particular non-neutralities to a firm's investment, employment, and sales decisions.

The Minnesota Department of Revenue (1993) examined the incidence of the state corporate income tax. The Department estimated that Minnesota consumers bear 39 percent of the tax, Minnesota labor bears 8 percent of the tax, and Minnesota capital bears 3 percent of the tax. Non-residents bear the rest of the tax. This incidence is roughly consistent with the relative weights then applied in Minnesota's apportionment formula and the theoretical mobility of the apportionment factors.

Technical details

This section presents details on how to calculate a company's state income tax liability under formulary apportionment. State profits are a function of total profits, the weight applied to each factor, and the share of each factor located in that state.[1] The formulation below shows the general case where each state may set the weight on the apportionment factor (including setting the weight to zero).

A firm's total profits, Π are distributed to each individual state, i, as shown below:

$$(1) \quad \Pi_i = [\alpha_i^k (K_i/K) + \alpha_i^L (L_i/L) + \alpha_i^S (S_i/S)] \Pi$$

where Π_i is post-apportionment state profits, K_i, L_i, and S_i are the company's property, payroll, and sales, respectively, in state i and K, L, and S are total property, payroll, and sales, respectively, over all states; and α_i^k, α_i^L and α_i^S, are the weights applied to the property, payroll, and sales shares in each state, respectively, where the sum of the weights on the factors is one, i.e., $\alpha_i^k + \alpha_i^L + \alpha_i^S = 1$. (Technically speaking, the sum of the weights must be less than or equal to one.)

The tax liability in any state is the product of the local tax rate, t_i, , and the post-apportionment profits, as shown below

$$(2) \quad T_i = t_i * \Pi_i$$

$$= t_i [\alpha_i^k (K_i/K) + \alpha_i^L (L_i/L) + \alpha_i^S (S_i/S)] \Pi$$

where T_i is tax revenue in state i and t_i is the statutory tax rate in state i.

The state corporate income tax may be represented as three separate taxes, each of which is levied as a share of the statutory rate on each factor in the formula. The property-related portion of the profits tax T_{ik} may be represented as:

$$(3) \quad T_{ik} = t_i [\alpha_i^k (K_i/K)] \Pi$$

If the apportionment formula weights the property factor by one-third, i.e., $\alpha_i^k = 1/3$, then the tax rate applied to state property is levied at one-third the statutory weight, i.e., $t_i \alpha_i^k$ Thus, if the statutory tax rate is nine percent and

Table 12. State apportionment tax rates, 2005.

	Maximum Tax Rate (%) (1)	Weight on Property Factor (2)	Rate Times Weight on Property (%) (3)
Alabama	6.5	1/3	2.17
Alaska	9.4	1/3	3.13
Arizona	6.968	1/4	1.74
Arkansas	6.5	1/4	1.63
California	8.84	1/4	2.21
Colorado	4.63	1/3	1.54
Connecticut	7.5	1/4	1.88
Delaware	8.7	1/3	2.90
Florida	5.5	1/4	1.38
Georgia	6.0	1/4	1.50
Hawaii	6.4	1/3	2.13
Idaho	7.6	1/4	1.9
Illinois	7.3	0	0
Indiana	8.5	1/4	2.13
Iowa	12.0	0	0
Kansas	4.0	1/3	1.33
Kentucky	8.25	1/4	2.06
Louisiana	8.0	1/4	2.00
Maine	8.93	1/4	2.23
Maryland	7.0	1/4	1.75
Massachusetts	9.5	1/4	2.38
Minnesota	9.8	1/8	1.23
Mississippi	5.0	1/3	1.67
Missouri	6.25	1/3	2.08
Montana	6.75	1/3	2.25
Nebraska	7.81	0	0
New Hampshire	8.5	1/4	2.13
New Jersey	9.0	1/4	2.25
New Mexico	7.6	1/4	1.90
New York	7.5	1/4	1.88
North Carolina	6.9	1/4	1.73
North Dakota	7.0	1/3	2.33
Ohio	8.5	1/5	1.70
Oklahoma	6.0	1/3	2.00
Oregon	6.6	1/10	0.66
Pennsylvania	9.99	1/5	2.00
Rhode Island	9.0	3/10	2.25
South Carolina	5.0	1/4	1.25
Tennessee	6.5	1/4	1.63
Utah	5.0	1/3	1.67
Vermont	9.75	1/3	3.25
Virginia	6.0	1/4	1.50
West Virginia	9.0	1/4	2.25
Wisconsin	7.9	1/4	1.98
District of Columbia	9.975	1/3	3.33
Average	7.54%	24.1%	1.80%

Note: Data are as of January 1, 2005. The rates listed are the maximum in states that offer graduated rates. The formulas listed are for general manufacturing businesses. Nevada, South Dakota, Washington, and Wyoming do not have state corporate income taxes. Michigan and Texas impose special types of taxes.
Source: Federation of Tax Administrators (2005).

the state weights the property factor by one-third, then the actual rate applied to the state property share falls to three percent. Representing the tax in this manner illustrates the strong incentive to eliminate the property factor from the formula since this move reduces the tax applied to property located in the state to zero.

Table 12 illustrates this effect. Column (1) shows the statutory tax rates, column (2) shows the weight on the property factor, and column (3) shows the apportionment tax rates on property for the states in 2005.

To show the incentives to modify the weight on the apportionment factor consider, for example, Iowa, Pennsylvania, and the District of Columbia. These three locations have nearly the same statutory tax rates, but they have very different apportionment tax rates. For example, Iowa has the highest statutory tax rate at 12 percent, but since it apportions solely on the basis of sales, its apportionment tax rate is zero.[2] Likewise, the statutory tax rates in both Pennsylvania and the District of Columbia are about 10 percent. However, since Pennsylvania weights the property factor by just 20 percent, its apportionment tax rate falls to 2 percent. By comparison, the District of Columbia, weights property by one-third so its apportionment tax rate is 3.33. These figures provide a simple illustration of how formulary apportionment reduces the tax rate applied to capital.

These calculations do not tell the entire story, however. Formulary apportionment with property as an apportionment factor affects a multistate firm's marginal investment in two distinct ways. To understand these effects, assume a firm moves some of its investment from a high tax area to a low tax area while keeping its total investment and profits fixed. This change in investment location has a direct effect and an indirect effect on the firm's tax burden. The direct effect arises because the firm is taxed at a lower average statutory rate.

Formulary apportionment introduces an indirect effect that is caused by the change in the share of profits taxed in each location. The sign of this indirect effect depends on the relationship between the apportionment tax rate, which is the product of the statutory tax rate and the weight on the factor in a location, and the capital-share weighted average apportionment tax rate over all locations. Thus, apportionment may create an additional "tax" or "subsidy" to new investment in a location. A tax arises if the state apportionment tax rate is greater than the overall average apportionment tax rate; a subsidy arises in the opposite case.

From a particular state's point of view, it may provide a subsidy to capital investment either by reducing the statutory tax rate or by reducing the weight on capital.[3] In the extreme case, the state may eliminate the capital factor from the formula by setting its weight to zero.

Box 1 illustrates these calculations.

Box 1. Derivation of marginal effective tax rates under apportionment[1]

To show how formulary apportionment transforms the state statutory tax rate, τ_i, into individual factor taxes, consider the calculations for state tax rate, τ_i, in state i, as shown below:

$$\text{(a)}\quad \tau_i \;=\; t_i\,[\alpha_i^k(K_i/K) + \alpha_i^L(Li/L) + \alpha_i^S(Si/S)]$$

where K_i, L_i, and S_i are property, payroll, and sales in state $_i$ and K, L, and S are total property, payroll, and sales over all states; and α_i^k, α_i^L, and α_i^S, are the weights on property, payroll, and sales shares in each state.

The tax rate levied on each factor share is shown as:

$$\text{(b1)}\quad \tau_i^k \;=\; t_i\,\alpha_i^k(Ki/K)$$

$$\text{(b2)}\quad \tau_i^L \;=\; t_i\,\alpha_i^L(Li/L)$$

$$\text{(b3)}\quad \tau_i^S \;=\; t_i\,\alpha_i^S(Si/S)$$

where equations (b1), (b2), and (b3), represent the individual apportionment factor taxes on property, payroll, and sales, respectively.

A multistate firm's overall tax rate is the sum of the individual factor taxes over all states:

$$\text{(c)}\quad \tau \;=\; \sum_i t_i\,\alpha_i^k(K_i/K) + \sum_i t_i\,\alpha_i^L(L_i/L) + \sum_i t_i\,\alpha_i^S(Si/S)$$

A change in the location of any of these factors changes the marginal apportionment tax rate.

Consider a firm that increases its investment in state i by shifting investment from other states so that total investment remains constant. This change gives the following expression for the marginal effective tax rate under apportionment:

$$\text{(d)}\quad \partial\tau/\partial K_i \;=\; (1/K)[\, t_i\,\alpha_i^k - \sum_{i\neq j} t_j\,\alpha_j^k\, K/\sum_{i\neq j} K_j\,]$$

Equation (d) can be positive or negative. For example, changing the marginal investment in a state increases the firm's overall tax rate if the state's apportionment tax on capital is greater than the weighted average tax on capital in all other states.

1. This exposition draws from Weiner (1994) and Goolsbee and Maydew (2000).

Expression (d) in Box 1 reveals certain incentives created by apportionment. First, a country where the apportionment tax rate is lower than the weighted average in all other countries has a negative effective marginal tax rate, i.e., it subsidizes new investment. Second, an individual country can maximize its investment incentive by setting its corporate tax rate to zero or by eliminating capital from the formula.[4] (If all countries follow this policy, then no country has an advantage.)

Table 13 calculates the apportionment tax rate and the effective marginal tax rate on capital for the EU Member States.[5] To highlight the impact of reducing the weight on capital, capital is the only factor in the formula in columns (1) and (2), while capital is weighted by one-fourth in columns (3) and (4).

Table 13. Calculations of EU tax rates under different capital factor, using the share of FDI stock in 2000 and tax rates in 2004

EU Member State	Weight on capital = 1		Weight on capital = ¼	
	Apportionment Tax Rate (1)	Effective Marginal Tax Rate (2)	Apportionment Tax Rate (3)	Effective Marginal Tax Rate (4)
Austria	34%	2.60%	8.5%	0.65%
Belgium	34	6.80	8.5	1.70
Czech Rep.	28	-3.83	7.0	-0.95
Denmark	30	-1.69	7.5	-0.42
Estonia	26	-6.15	6.5	-1.53
Finland	29	-2.86	7.25	-0.71
France	35	6.75	8.75	1.68
Germany	38	9.28	9.5	2.32
Greece	35	3.00	8.75	0.75
Hungary	16	-15.97	4.0	-3.99
Ireland	12.5	-29.69	3.13	-7.42
Italy	33	2.32	8.25	0.58
Latvia	15	-17.16	3.75	-4.29
Lithuania	15	-17.16	3.75	-4.29
Netherlands	30	10.07	8.63	2.51
Poland	19	-12.92	4.75	-3.23
Portugal	27.5	-4.19	6.88	-1.04
Slovakia	19	-13.13	4.75	-3.28
Slovenia	25	-7.13	6.25	-1.78
Spain	35	4.78	8.75	1.19
Sweden	28	-3.45	7.0	-0.86
UK	30	2.09	7.5	0.52
Average	27.20%	-3.98%	6.80%	-1.00%
Maximum	38	10.07	9.50	2.51
Minimum	12.5	-29.69	3.13	-7.42
Std deviation	7.80	10.21	1.97	2.55

Source: Foreign direct investment data are from Eurostat (2001). FDI data are not available for Cyprus, Luxembourg, and Malta. Tax rates are from Copenhagen Economics (2004).

Column (1) shows the apportionment tax rate when capital is the only apportionment factor. Since the weight on capital is one in this case, the apportionment tax rate equals the statutory tax rate. Column (2) shows the effective marginal tax rate calculated from expression (d) in Box 1 using the share of foreign direct investment stocks in each country as a proxy for the property factor.[6] Countries where the apportionment tax rate is below the weighted average tax rate have a negative effective marginal tax rate, and vice versa.

These calculations show that the ranking of countries in terms of their tax burden depends on the formula. To illustrate, compare the UK with Denmark. These countries have the same statutory tax rate, but Denmark's effective tax rate is lower than the UK's. This outcome occurs because the UK already has a lot of capital relative to Denmark. A firm can reduce its overall average tax rate by investing in Denmark rather than in the UK even though the statutory tax rate is the same in the two countries.[7]

Columns (3) and (4) repeat the analysis, but reduce the weight on capital to one-fourth, as in the double-weighted sales formula. A formula that uses factors in addition to capital reduces the apportionment tax rate levied on capital. For example, the average tax rate when capital is the only factor equals just over 27 percent, but if capital is weighted by one-fourth, the average tax rate on capital falls to 6.8 percent.

The level and variation of marginal effective tax rates also fall under the new formula (compare column (4) with column (2)). Since it is the variation in cross-border tax burdens that may cause the greatest distortions to capital location, the narrowing of the cross-country spread in tax burdens may improve the efficiency of capital allocation in the European Union. This outcome may be one of the most important benefits of introducing formulary apportionment into the European Union.

7.2   EMPIRICAL EVIDENCE

The empirical research on formulary apportionment has addressed four broad questions: (1) Do variations in the apportionment formula affect the relative factor choices of multijurisdictional firms? (2) Do changes in the apportionment formulae affect state investment and employment? (3) Do firms shift factors to take advantage of tax differentials, i.e., do they engage in tax planning? (4) Does cross-provincial variation in tax rates and credits affect investment spending and income shifting? The evidence from the empirical studies indicates that the answer to all four questions is: "Yes." Apportionment affects the factor choices of firms, the amount and location of investment and employment, and income shifting.

Some of these results arise from differences in the weights applied to the apportionment factors and may not appear relevant for the EU where it is presumed Member States will adopt a common formula. However, a reduction in the weight on a factor has effects similar to a reduction in the statutory tax rate. These results illustrate how changes in statutory tax rates within a formulary apportionment system may affect EU business activity.[8]

Impact on factor choices

The U.S. states provide a good environment for understanding how formulary apportionment may affect factor choices. For example, if as shown in theory, the apportionment formula effectively acts as a tax on the factors in the formula, then, for example, industries located in states with relatively heavy weights on capital, would be expected to be relatively more labor-intensive than the same industry located in a state with a lighter burden on capital. The fact that the observed capital-labor ratios for the same industry in different states are quite different suggests that the apportionment formula may have affected the relative factor choices.

To test this hypothesis, Weiner (1994) constructed state and industry-specific measures of the cost of capital and the cost of labor for 15 industries in 35 states for 1977. Using a cross-section of state industrial data and controlling for industry and state effects, Weiner finds that industries located in states with a lower cost of capital relative to labor have a greater capital-labor ratio. However, apportionment is not the main cause of those variations. Even though states changed their formulae over time, they generally maintained equal weights on the property and payroll factors. With equal factor weights, even after accounting for additional differences in state tax rates and state tax practices, there is insufficient cross-state variation in the relative cost of capital to explain the wide cross-state variation in the relative capital-intensity within an industry across the states.

Investment, employment, and sales effects

Other empirical studies examine how changes in the apportionment formula affect investment, employment and sales. These studies generally find that changes in the apportionment formula have a significant influence on state investment and employment.

Beginning in about 1980, the states began reducing the weights on the property and payroll factor and increasing the weight on the destination-based sales factor. For example, in 1980, 45 states plus the District of Columbia regularly applied the evenly weighted three-factor formula. However, following a Supreme Court decision in 1978 sanctioning the use of a single-factor sales formula, many states began moving toward a "super-weighted" sales factor.[9] As a result, by 2005, only 11 states (plus the District of Columbia) continue to apply the Massachusetts formula, and the double-weighted sales formula has replaced the equally weighted three-factor formula as the most common apportionment formula.[10]

Many states justify increasing the weight on the sales-factor as a way to encourage companies to locate production facilities in the state. As discussed below, states that apportion solely on the basis of destination-based sales encourage firms to produce in the state and sell out of state.

In an early examination of this policy, Weiner (1994) estimates how state changes in tax rates and in the apportionment formula between 1982 and 1990 affect investment spending.[11] States that reduce the property factor weight, all else equal, stimulate additional state investment spending. The effect is statistically significant, but empirically not very large.

Using pooled state data for 1983 to 1996, Gupta and Hofman (2003) find that new capital expenditures fall as the tax burden on capital increases. The tax policy variables have a statistically significant influence, but their economic significance is almost negligible, implying that the impact of the policy change may be smaller than state policymakers anticipate.

Changes in the apportionment formula also affect employment. Using a panel of state data from 1978 through 1994, Goolsbee and Maydew (2000) find that manufacturing employment increases in states that reduce the weight on the payroll factor. However, since the employment gains in one state are offset by employment losses in other states, the country as a whole would be better off if the states used the same formula than if they used competing formulae.

Empirical evidence under a common formula and tax base

Evidence from Canada, where the provinces apply a common formula, provides two very useful lessons for the European Union. First, provinces can compete for investment by cutting tax rates or by offering post-apportionment tax credits while still using a common formula and common tax base. Second, since consolidation is effectively optional, provincial income shifting possibilities arise through adjustments in the corporate form.

Using a panel of provincial data from 1962 to 1989, Weiner (1994) finds that tax policy is highly effective at the provincial level. Reductions in either the provincial cost of capital or in the provincial statutory tax rate increase provincial investment. The impact of these changes became particularly noticeable after Canada introduced investment incentives for the manufacturing sector in the 1970s. The analysis also shows that provinces engage in a tax rate competition for investment. Provinces that reduce the tax burden on investment, either through rate cuts or through tax credits, stimulate new investment, holding tax rates in competing provinces fixed.

These results have potentially powerful implications for the European Union. They show that even within a system with a common tax base and common formula, as long as the Member States retain the ability to set tax rates (and/or grant post-apportionment tax credits), they have the flexibility to use tax policy to stimulate new investment spending. Thus, EU businesses gain the benefits of reduced compliance costs while EU Member States maintain the advantages of controlling important elements of their company tax policy.

Evidence from Canada, however, suggests that the Member States may need to implement anti-abuse measures if the EU adopts a common tax base without consolidation. For example, using provincial tax and investment data from 1986 to 1999, Mintz and Smart (2004) explore the tax planning opportunities that arise under the separate-entity system used in the provinces. Because firms that operate through legally-separate subsidiaries in other provinces do not consolidate their income into a single tax base and, thus, are not subject to apportionment, they may shift expenses across provinces through strategic lending and borrowing.[12] Mintz and Smart conclude that since Canada does not require corporate groups to consolidate their accounts, "a number of tax planning devices are essentially unrestricted for firms that incorporate separately in separate provinces."

Klassen and Shackelford (1998) examine how companies in the United States and Canada re-locate their sales, the "purported primary method of subnational tax avoidance," to reduce their tax burden. They find evidence consistent with corporations shifting their tax bases to tax-favorable jurisdictions. Manufacturing companies strategically structure their shipments to reduce sales reported to locations with relatively heavy taxation of sales.

Theoretical studies

Finally, the evidence from a series of theoretical papers confirms the importance of using a common formula. Anand and Sansing (2000) show that social welfare is higher under any common formula, no matter how defined, than under non-uniform formulae. Edmiston (2002) shows the adverse consequences from non-cooperation at the state level in choosing an apportionment formula. Omer and Shelley (2004) find that subnational competition for mobile business capital, employment, and sales leads state governments to engage in an "apportionment" competition with other states.

In summing up the implications of these studies in terms of choosing an apportionment formula, the European Union may wish to consider the views Thomas S. Adams expressed in 1922: "Everybody knows that we and our successors for one hundred years are not going to settle this problem of allocating with scientific accuracy . . . Any uniform rule is better than the existing situation. Now, let us get a rule, and then all get behind it and try to get that one rule adopted."[13] From the viewpoint of the European Union, one can hardly doubt the importance of gaining agreement on a formula that distributes income fairly and reasonably across the Member States.

7.3 REVENUE EFFECTS UNDER DIFFERENT FORMULAE

Although the actual revenue distribution depends on the formula, the state experience shows that a formula that includes multiple factors generally does not have significant revenue consequences. For example, based on a statewide analysis of the revenue impact of different formulae, the U.S. Congressional Willis Committee (1964) concluded that "...the choice among . . . formulas is not an issue involving great amounts of money." Two decades later, Sheffrin and Fulcher (1984) examined the revenue consequences for various formulae and also found that there generally is no formula that a state prefers over all periods. For example, suppose a state's objective is to maximize revenue. To achieve this goal, nearly one in three states would have had to change its formula in 1980 if it wished to continue to apply the formula that maximized revenue in 1977. It is clear that it is not possible, nor advisable, for the states to change their policies that frequently.

Actual tax return data are the best source to show how policy changes affect state revenues. Meyer and Oshiro (1996) use tax return data to estimate the revenue consequences when Arizona moved to a double-weighted sales formula in 1991. In the first full year the policy was in effect, tax payments had fallen for roughly 40 percent of corporations with the new formula, but the distribution of the tax changes was widely dispersed across industries. The typical electronic equipment company had an 11 percent tax cut while a typical company in the food products industry had a 31 percent tax increase. The study does not report the distribution of the factors for these companies, but based on the changes in tax payments, it appears, in general, that the food industry produces and sells locally while the electronic industry produces locally and sells nationally.

7.4   THEORETICAL ANALYSIS OF FORMULARY APPORTIONMENT

To conclude the economic analysis, this section examines the theoretical studies of how formulary apportionment may affect tax competition, investment, and efficiency. Many economists have developed theoretical models to demonstrate how formulary apportionment may affect investment, employment, and tax competition. Following McLure (1980), the efforts continued with Gordon and Wilson (1986) who examine how formulary apportionment affects the equilibrium behavior of individual firms and states. They highlight their main results with a single-factor property formula.[14]

Gordon and Wilson first show that formulary apportionment encourages cross-border mergers. Suppose a profitable firm doing business in a high-tax state merges with a firm in a low-tax state. Following the merger, it apportions part of its profits from the high-tax state to the low-tax state and, thus, reduces its total tax payments. Formulary apportionment encourages cross-border mergers of profitable firms until all firms face the same average tax rate.

This result also suggests that tax competition is greater under formulary apportionment than under separate accounting. Under both systems, when a country increases its tax rate, firms have an incentive to move capital to lower tax locations. However, formulary apportionment introduces a second effect. The firm can reduce the share of its income taxed at the now higher rate by re-adjusting the share of investment in each location. This re-allocation effect does not exist under separate accounting; thus, formulary apportionment increases tax competition relative to separate accounting.

Finally, states that apportion solely on the basis of destination-based sales encourage firms to produce in the state and sell out of the state. Suppose a state applies a sales-only formula. An out-of-state firm that opens a factory in the state will not owe any additional income taxes to the state. However, some of its total tax base will now be apportioned to the state so that the share of its total income in the other states falls, thus reducing its total tax payments. Firms have an incentive to produce in the state but sell elsewhere.

These results have generally been accepted as the standard wisdom. However, some recent studies that impose different assumptions --- such as the ability to shift income under separate accounting using transfer prices --- find that formulary apportionment may not necessarily lead to more tax competition than separate accounting.

Tax competition and fiscal externalities

As discussed in chapter 2, the econometric evidence generally shows that multinational enterprises appear able to adjust their transfer prices to shift income to tax-favored locations. Under formulary apportionment with consolidated base taxation, the opportunity to shift income through manipulating transfer prices disappears because intercompany transactions are eliminated when calculating the consolidated tax base.[15] This fact has led many analysts to view formulary apportionment as a solution to the transfer pricing problem that arises under separate accounting. However, formulary apportionment introduces new distortions to investment and employment decisions so that it is not clear, a priori, whether one system is preferable to another system from a welfare point of view.

With the European Union considering moving to formulary apportionment, many economists have re-examined the theoretical impacts of formulary apportionment. For example, Sorensen (2004) examines how a switch from separate accounting to formulary apportionment might affect tax competition within the European Union.[16]

Under Sorensen's model, tax competition may not necessarily be greater under formulary apportionment than under separate accounting. For example, if firms do not re-adjust the share of investment in each location, say because investment is equally sensitive to domestic and foreign tax rate increases, a domestic tax increase has no "secondary" positive spillover effect on investment in the foreign country. Foreign tax revenue unambiguously falls since total investment declines without an offsetting increase in the share of investment in the foreign country.

Although a domestic tax increase tends to have offsetting effects in the foreign country under separate accounting (revenue falls, but investment rises), a domestic tax increase in a formulary apportionment system may cause both revenue and investment to fall in the foreign country. Since the domestic country does not take these negative effects into account, tax rates will be too high under formulary apportionment and there will be less tax competition under formulary apportionment than under separate accounting.

Nielsen, Raimondos-Møller, and Schjelderup (2001) examine tax spillovers under separate accounting and formulary apportionment under competitive market conditions. In this model, whenever countries face the threat of tax base flight, either because transfer pricing manipulation is not very costly under separate accounting or because pure profits are large under formulary apportionment, countries face pressure to keep tax rates low.

For example, under separate accounting, companies may shift income by manipulating their transfer prices. As the cost of transfer pricing increases, the amount of transfer pricing manipulation falls, and the pressure on countries to keep tax rates low falls.

Under formulary apportionment, companies may shift income by relocating their factor shares. As the size of pure profits increases, the incentive to shift profits increases, and the pressure on countries to keep tax rates low increases. Combining these two effects shows that if transfer pricing is costly, say because countries impose large penalties for improper transfer pricing, and if pure profits are large, formulary apportionment will increase tax competition relative to separate accounting.

As an extension, suppose that transfer pricing is costly and the firm can not alter the location of the apportionment factors. In this case, the effects on tax competition are ambiguous. Whether this capital immobility arises because transfer pricing is costly or because the apportionment factor is fixed, the pressure on countries to keep tax rates low under either system is reduced. It is not clear, therefore, which system leads to relatively greater tax competition.

Other studies have examined various features of the apportionment formula and tax base. If the European Union adopts the Canadian-style formula that does not include a capital factor, Wellisch (2004) reasons that traditional tax competition does not arise.[17] Wellisch also explains that a formula based entirely on labor shifts the full tax burden to labor (or, more generally, to any other immobile factor included in the formula, such as land). By contrast, if the formula includes sales, then both local consumers and foreign consumers are likely to bear some portion of the tax. This result highlights the general view that a multiple-factor formula has advantages over a single factor formula.

Assuming that countries agree to use the same formula, Pethig and Wagener (2004) examine how tax competition varies under different formulae. Tax competition will generally be stronger the more sensitive factor shares are to tax rate differences. Since labor is assumed to be the least mobile factor, at least in the short run, tax competition is likely to be lower under this formula than under formulae that include property and sales factors.

The tax base may also be an important element to consider. Kolmar and Wagener (2004) find that although the amount of tax competition is independent of the tax base under separate accounting, the tax base and the formula simultaneously affect tax competition under apportionment.

Mintz and Weiner (2003) consider the efficiency aspects of the European Commission's specific proposals. As long as tax rates continue to differ across Member States, economic inefficiencies arise under formulary apportionment. It is not clear whether the inefficiencies introduced through formulary apportionment (e.g., distortions through shifting the locations of factors) are empirically more important compared to the inefficiencies that are removed (e.g., the differences in tax bases.).

Gérard and Weiner (2003) and Gérard (2005) examine a situation of formulary apportionment and cross-border loss offsetting in a model with uncertainty. The uncertainty arises because companies may have losses in one jurisdiction and profits in another jurisdiction. If the EU introduces cross-border loss offsetting, a multinational company will be able to offset profits in one jurisdiction with losses from another jurisdiction and Member State revenue may fall as it absorbs losses from other jurisdictions. Formulary apportionment, however, has the benefit of partially insuring governments against these negative impacts. As long as the firm is profitable overall, Member States will receive some income under formulary apportionment. Governments are, therefore, eager to attract foreign investment since formulary apportionment acts as a type of insurance against a bad outcome, so they continue to set competitive income tax rates.

Notes

1. Note that the definitions of total profits and the factor totals depend on how the taxable group is defined. For example, compared with water's edge consolidation, if the group includes worldwide operations, the factor shares will decrease so that a smaller share of total income will be apportioned to the state; the amount of total profits will generally increase when the composition of the group expands geographically. However, total profits will decrease under worldwide consolidation if the company has losses in its foreign operations. The fact that worldwide consolidation (combination) can reduce a company's tax liability explains why many companies choose worldwide combination in the states that make this option available (for an illustration, see the discussion in Coffill (1993) of the changes to California's water's edge election legislation in 1993.). See also *Caterpillar Tractor Co., et al. v. Daniel J. Lenckos*, 84 Ill. 2d 102 (1981) upholding the company's right to file on a worldwide combined basis in Illinois.

2. Since states taxes are deductible from federal taxes, the actual state tax rate equals ((1-federal rate) * state tax rate * weight on property). A reduction in the federal rate, therefore, increases the tax rate in all the states.

3. While a state may view these policies as providing a state subsidy, within the United States as a whole, Mieszkowski and Morgan (1984) and Mieszkowski and Zodrow (1985) show that these local effects tend to offset one another. Labor, capital, and consumers in the high tax states subsidize labor, capital and consumers in the low tax states. At the national level, however, the local taxes initially increase the cost of equity capital in all locations, which discourages the use of capital and reduces the after-tax return on capital relative to labor, thus driving down the return to equity nationwide.

4. As discussed in section 7.2, the states recognize that as more and more states reduce the weight on capital and increase the weight on sales, the less attractive their own state becomes for investment if they remain with the Massachusetts formula. Furthermore, the gain is largest for the states that move first. Thus, the states are engaged in a race towards a destination-based sales-only apportionment formula.

5. For simplicity, these calculations assume that profit rates are identical across factors. See Weiner (1994) for estimates on the U.S. states that relax this condition.

6. As with the calculations shown in Chapter 2, these data may not represent the capital data that the European Union may use in its apportionment formula.

7. As discussed in section 7.4, formulary apportionment encourages such cross-border investment.

8. One major difference, however, is that a change in the tax rate affects all companies while a change in the formula only affects companies doing business in more than one location.

9. See *Moorman v. Bair*, 437 U.S. 267 (1978) upholding the single-factor sales formula. In this case, the Moorman Manufacturing Company, an Illinois corporation, manufactured animal feeds in Illinois that it sold in Iowa and elsewhere. Iowa apportioned income solely on the basis of sales and gross receipts. Illinois used the Massachusetts formula.

10. As of 2005, two additional states joined Iowa in apportioning solely on the basis of sales, and Oregon will use this formula as of 2008. See the Federation of Tax Administrators website for current company tax rates and apportionment formulae (www.taxadmin.org).

11. States that change the apportionment formula often change the tax rate at the same time. For example, although the average statutory rate rose nearly one percentage point in the states that moved to the double weighted sales formula in the 1990s, the average apportionment tax rate fell by 1.6 percentage points during that period. Within these states, the average weight on the property factor fell by about one-third. In addition, if states increase the tax rate at the same time that they reduce the factor weight, the apportionment tax rate may remain constant.

12. As discussed in Chapter 5, the ability of firms to shift income to legally-separate out of state subsidiaries led California to extend the formulary apportionment system to the "unitary" business.

13. See *Proceedings of the National Tax Association* (1922). Adams made this comment at a state tax meeting, but the importance of applying a uniform rule applied with equal force at the international level, where Adams was also working.

14. Capital is completely mobile across states while labor is completely immobile. Firms operate in competitive markets and earn zero economic profits in the long run. Under these assumptions, pre-tax profits must rise to offset any increase in the firm's tax burden.

15. Firms can still engage in transfer pricing to alter the location of the apportionment factors or to change the amount of income attributed to the taxable group.

16. Sorensen extends the model developed by Nielsen, Raimondos-Moller, and Schjelderup (2001). This model allows for transfer pricing and has a variable global capital stock.

17. For evidence that tax competition does arise, see the empirical evidence from Weiner (1994) and Mintz and Smart (2004) reported earlier.

Chapter 8

CONCLUSION: IMPLEMENTING FORMULARY APPORTIONMENT IN THE EUROPEAN UNION

In the early 20th century, nations considered, and rejected, formulary apportionment as the international method for distributing a multinational company's taxable income across national borders. They gave many reasons for this decision: Accounting standards differed across countries. Countries had their own currencies, they imposed currency exchange controls, and tax and tariff barriers surrounded their borders. Companies generally did business in a single country. Companies that expanded their business across national borders engaged in simple, easy-to-price transactions with their affiliates. Since companies organized their operations within a single country, it made sense to apply a tax system that calculated profits based on company's separate accounts in each country.

At that same time, however, the U.S. states considered, and adopted, formulary apportionment as the method for distributing a multistate company's taxable income across state borders. The states gave many reasons for this decision. The states used the same accounting system and currency, and there were no tax or tariff walls around their borders. Many companies did business in more than one state, and many of them had a value that began with manufacture in one state and sales in other states. In short, multistate companies operated with a nationwide focus, not a statewide focus.

In the early 20th century, nations went in the direction of separate-entity accounting, and the U.S. states went in the direction of formulary apportionment. This split was logical at the time. The international tax experts had no need to design a company tax system appropriate for a group of economically integrated, but politically sovereign countries.

Much has changed at the international level since then, especially in the European Union. The economic integration has led the European Commission to suggest that the EU Member States re-consider how they tax multinational enterprises. Specifically, the Commission proposes that EU multinational enterprises have the opportunity to calculate a common tax base at the EU level and use a common formula to distribute the common tax base to the Member States for taxation at local rates.

The current separate-entity method with arm's length prices was appropriate at a time when EU companies generally did business at the local level and their transactions with related entities involved transfers of tangible goods for which market prices were readily available. In the 21st century, however, that form of taxation reflects neither the structure of EU businesses nor the nature of their transactions. In the Single Market, EU companies operate at the EU level. They are pan-European businesses.

The nature of cross-border intercompany transfers has also changed. Multinational enterprises no longer primarily transfer basic goods for which arm's length prices are readily available. Their internal transfers increasingly involve transfers of difficult-to-value intangible property (patents, copyrights, trademarks, etc.). EU multinational enterprises have a value as an integrated enterprise that exceeds the value of the sum of their individual parts. Enterprises no longer need a physical presence in a location to derive significant income from their economic presence in that location.

Tax authorities face difficult challenges enforcing the separate-entity method. Companies are adept at devising ways to shift income inappropriately and move income from high-tax into low-tax jurisdictions (and to move losses from low-tax into high-tax jurisdictions). Many of these techniques involve manipulating transfer prices, changing the form of financing, and altering the corporate structure.

Tax authorities have reacted by imposing strict enforcement measures, increasing documentation requirements, and penalizing taxpayers when they fail to comply with these requirements. Preserving the national tax base under the separate-entity method with the arm's length principle has become a burdensome compliance exercise, for taxpayers and tax authorities alike.

The U.S. states and Canadian provinces applied separate accounting at a time when companies generally operated locally. But, Canada dropped the separate accounting method for permanent establishments because "it was a headache and no one was using it." The U.S. states moved away from separate accounting because "there would be no practical way to determine what income of a company is earned within one state as opposed to within another."

Formulary apportionment does not eliminate Member State tax sovereignty. To the contrary, the local tax rate remains a highly effective fiscal tool under formulary apportionment even in a system with a common formula and common tax base. As long as the Member States remain able to set their own tax rates, which is a fundamental element of the European Commission's strategy, each Member State will be able to remain competitive in the drive to stimulate new investment and employment.

EU Member States and EU businesses now appreciate that formulary methods are often the best way to split profits for tax purposes within a multinational enterprise. Apportioning profits on the basis of a firm-specific profit-split formula is a move toward apportioning profits on the basis of a common profit-split formula.

The EU Member States may wish to focus on designing a tax system that is best suited for the Single Market. Although the EU political structure differs greatly from the structures in the United States and Canada, from a business viewpoint, all three economies are integrated markets. The U.S. and Canada use a tax system designed for an integrated market. Perhaps the European Union should also use a tax system designed for an integrated market.

BIBLIOGRAPHY

Altshuler, Rosanne and Timothy Goodspeed (2002), "Follow the leader? Evidence on European and U.S. tax competition," mimeo, Hunter College.

Amerkhail, Valerie (2000), "Arm's Length or Formulary Apportionment? Sometimes the Best Choice is Both," 9 *Tax Management Transfer Pricing. No. 13 Special Report*, Washington, D.C.: Bureau of National Affairs, pp. S25-S35.

Anand, Bharat N. and Richard Sansing (2000), "The weighting game: formula apportionment as an instrument of public policy, 53 *National Tax Journal* 2, pp. 183-99.

Arnold, Brian J. (2003), "Threshold Requirements for Taxing Business Profits Under Tax Treaties," in Brian J. Arnold, Jacques Sasseville, and Eric M. Zolt, eds., *The Taxation of Business Profits Under Tax Treaties*, Ontario: Canadian Tax Foundation, pp. 55-108.

Avi-Yonah, Reuven (1995), "The Rise and Fall of Arm's Length: A Study in the Evolution of U.S. International Taxation," 15 *Virginia Tax Review* 1, pp. 89-159.

Bartelsman, Eric and Roel Beestma (2003), "Why Pay More? Corporate Tax Avoidance Through Transfer Pricing in OECD Countries," 87 *Journal of Public Economics* No. 9-10, pp. 2225-2252.

Bird, Richard and Donald S. Brean (1986), "The Interjurisdictional Allocation of Income and the Unitary Taxation Debate," 34 *Canadian Tax Journal* 6, pp. 1377-1416.

Brown, Robert D. (1984), "Canada-U.S. Tax Issues: The Tax Treaty, Unitary Taxation, and the Future," International Tax Planning Feature (May-June 1984), 32 *Canadian Tax Journal*, pp. 547-71.

Carroll, Mitchell B. (1933), *Taxation of Foreign and National Enterprises Volume IV – Methods of Allocating Taxable Income (Carroll Report)*, League of Nations Document No. C.425.M.217(b). IIA.

Clausing, Kimberly A. (2003), "Tax-motivated Transfer Pricing and U.S. Intrafirm Trade Prices," 87 *Journal of Public Economics* No. 9-10, pp. 2207-23.

Coffill, Eric J. (1993), "A Kinder, Gentler 'Water's Edge' Election: California Wards Off Threats of U.K. Retaliation as Part of Comprehensive Business Incentive Tax Package," 61 *Tax Notes* No. 4, pp. 477-87.

Commission of the European Communities (2005a), "Court Cases in the Field of, or of Particular Interest for, Direct Taxation," Taxation and Customs Union.

_____ (2005b), "Losses in Cross-Border Situations," April.

_____ (2004a), "A Common Consolidated EU Corporate Tax Base," Non-paper presented to informal Ecofin Council, 10 and 11 September 2004.

_____ (2004b), *European Tax Survey,* Working Paper No 3/2004, Directorate-General Taxation and Customs Union, Luxembourg: Official Publications of the European Communities.

_____ (2003a), "An Internal Market without company tax obstacles. Achievements, ongoing initiatives and remaining challenges," COM(2003) 726 (24 November 2003), Brussels.

_____ (2003b), "Internal Market Scoreboard No. 12," 5 May 2003, Brussels.

_____ (2002), *Company Taxation in the Internal Market,* Commission staff working paper, Office of Official Publications of the European Communities: Luxembourg. (Originally published as SEC (2001) 1681, 23 October 2001).

_____ (2001), "Towards an Internal Market without tax obstacles. A strategy for providing companies with a consolidated corporate tax base for the EU-wide activities," Communication from the Commission to the Council, the European Parliament and the Economic and Social Committee, COM(2001) 582 final, Brussels, 23 October 2001.

_____ (2000), *European Economy Mergers and Acquisitions.* Supplement A, 5/6, Luxembourg: Official Publications of the European Communities.

_____ (1992a), *Report of the Committee of Independent Experts on Company Taxation* (the Ruding Report), Luxembourg: Office of Official Publications of the European Communities.

_____ (1992b), "Subsequent to the conclusions of the Ruding Committee indicating guidelines on company taxation linked to the further development of the internal market," Communication to the Council and to Parliament, SEC (92) 118, 26 June 1992.

_____ (1990), *Guidelines on Company Taxation,* Commission Communication to Parliament and the Council (20 April), COM(90) 601 final.

Copenhagen Economics (2004), *Economic effects of tax cooperation in an enlarged European Union,* Final Report, Copenhagen.

Culbertson, Robert E. (1995), "A Rose by any other name: Smelling the flowers at the OECD's (Last) resort," 11 *Tax Notes Int'l* 370 (Aug. 7, 1995).

Dagostino, Emily (2004), "Is New Vermont Law a Sign of a Combined Reporting Comeback?" 34 *State Tax Notes* 7 (4 October 2004).

Dennehy, Edward K. and Stephen G. and Ehrlich (2004), "PICking Away at Passive Investment Companies: States Enact Legislation to Curtail Revenue Losses," 33 State Tax Notes 777 (Sept. 13, 2004).

Devgun, Derek (1996), "International Fiscal Wars for the Twenty-First Century: An Assessment of Tax-Based Trade Retaliation," 27 *Law and Policy in International Business* 2, pp. 353-421.

Durst, Michael C. and Robert E. Culbertson (2003), "Clearing Away and Sand: Retrospective Methods and Prospective Documentation in Transfer Pricing Today," 57 *Tax Law Review* No. 1, pp. 37-136.

Eden, Lorraine, M. Tina Dacin and William P. Wan (2001), "Standards across borders: Cross-border diffusion of the arm's length standard in North America," *Accounting, Organizations and Society* 26, pp. 1-23.

Edmiston, Kelly (2002), "Strategic Apportionment of the State Corporate Income Tax," 55 *Nat'l Tax Journal* 2, pp. 239-62.

_____(2001), "A Single-Factor Sales Apportionment Formula in the State of Georgia," Georgia State University, mimeo.

Ernst & Young (1997, 1999, 2001, 2003), *Global Transfer Pricing Survey.*

Eurostat (2004), *Structures of the taxation systems in the European Union. Data 1995-2002,* Luxembourg: Office for Official Publications of the European Communities.

_____ (2003), *European Business. Facts and Figures. Data 1991-2001*. Luxembourg: Office for Official Publications of the European Communities.

_____ (2001), *European Union Foreign Direct Investment Yearbook 2000,* Luxembourg: Office for Official Publications of the European Communities.

Federation of Tax Administrators (2005), "State Apportionment of Corporate Income," mimeo. See www.taxadmin.org.

Ferguson, Fred E. (1986), "Worldwide Unitary Taxation: The End Appears Near," 4 *Journal of State Taxation* 4, pp. 241-59.

Fernandez, Albertina (1996), "Dorgan Blasts Arm's Length Transfer Pricing Method," 13 *Tax Notes Int'l* 26, (23 December 1996), pp. 2081-83.

Finkenzeller, Mark and Christoph Spengel (2004), "Measuring the Effective Levels of Company Taxation in the New Member States: A Quantitative Analysis," European Commission Taxation Working Paper No. 7, Luxembourg: Office for Official Publications of the European Communities.

Fox, William F. and LeAnn Luna (2002), "State Corporate Tax Revenue Trends: Causes and Possible Solutions," 55 *National Tax Journal* 3 (September 2002), pp. 491-508.

Franchise Tax Board of California (2002a), *2002 Guidelines for Corporations Filing a Combined Report* State of California.

_____ (2002b), *Form 100W, Water's Edge Booklet,* State of California.

Gérard, Marcel (2005), "Multijurisdictional firms and governments' strategies under alternative tax designs," Catholic University of Mons, Belgium, mimeo.

_____ and Joann M. Weiner (2003), "Cross-Border Loss Offset and Formulary Apportionment: How do they Affect Multijurisdictional Firm Investment Spending and Interjurisdictional Tax Competition?" CESIfo Working Paper No. 1004, Munich.

Gerstenberg, Charles W. (1931), "Allocation of Business Income," *Proceedings of the 24th Annual Conference of the National Tax Association.*

Goldsworth, John (1989), "Tax Harmonization in the EEC and 1992," 1 *Tax Notes International* 587.

Goolsbee, Austan and Edward Maydew (2000), "Coveting they neighbor's manufacturing: the dilemma of state income apportionment," 75 *Journal of Public Economics* 1, pp. 125-43.

Gordon, Roger and John D. Wilson (1986), "An examination of multijurisdictional corporate income taxation under formula apportionment," 54 *Econometrica* 6, pp. 1357-73.

Gorter, Joeri and Ruud A. de Mooij (2001), "Capital income taxation in Europe: Trends and tradeoffs," Central Planning Bureau, Netherlands Bureau for Economic Policy Analysis, The Hague.

Graetz, Michael J. and Michael M. O'Hear (1997), "The 'Original Intent' of U.S. International Taxation," 46 *Duke Law Journal*, pp. 1021-1109.

Gresik, Thomas A. (2001), "The Taxing Task of Taxing Transnationals," 34 *Journal of Economic Literature* 3 (September 2001), pp. 800-38.

Grubert, Harry (2003), "Intangible Income, Intercompany Transactions, Income Shifting, and the Choice of Location," 56 *National Tax Journal* No. 1, Part 2, pp. 221-42.

_____ (1997), "Another look at the low taxable income of foreign-controlled companies," OTA Paper 74, U.S. Department of the Treasury, Washington, D.C.

_____, Timothy Goodspeed, and Deborah Swenson (1993), "Explaining the Low Taxable Income of Foreign-Controlled Companies in the United States," in Alberto Giovannini, R. Glenn Hubbard and Joel Slemrod, eds., *studies in International Taxation* (1993), Chicago and London: University of Chicago Press.

Guariglia, Michael A., David J. Shipley, and Open Weaver Banks (2005), "Exceptions to Interest Addback Requirements for Related-Member Interest and Intangible Expenses," 37 *State Tax Notes 355* (1 Aug. 2005).

Gupta, Sanjay and Mary Ann Hofmann (2003), "The Effect of State Income Tax Apportionment and Tax Incentives on New Capital Expenditures," *Journal of American Taxation Association* 25 (Supplement), pp. 1-25.

Healy, John C. (2001), *Multistate Corporate Tax Guide. Vol. 1. Corporate Income Tax*, New York: Panel Publishers.

Hellerstein, Jerome R. (1995), "Geoffrey and the Physical Presence Nexus Requirement of Quill," 8 *State Tax notes* 671 (13 February 1995).

_____ (1968), "Recent developments in state tax apportionment and the circumscription of unitary business," XXI *National Tax Journal* No. 4, pp. 487-503

_____ and Walter Hellerstein (1998, cum. Supp. 2005), *State Taxation*, 3rd ed., Boston: Warren, Gorham, and Lamont.

_____ and ----- (2005), *State and Local Taxation. Cases and Materials.* 8th ed., West Publishing Co.

Hellerstein, Walter (2005), "The case for formulary apportionment," 12 *International transfer pricing journal* No. 3, pp. 103-111

_____ (2001), "The Business-Nonbusiness Income Distinction and the Case for Its Abolition," 21 *State Tax Notes* 725 (Sept. 3, 2001).

_____ and Charles E. McLure, Jr. (2004), "The European Commission's Report on Company Income Taxation: What the EU Can Learn from the Experience of the US States," 11 *International Tax and Public Finance* 2, pp. 199-220.

Keesling, Frank M. and John S. Warren (1960), "The Unitary Concept in the Allocation of Income," 12 *The Hastings Law Journal* (August 1960), pp. 42-64.

Klassen, Kenneth J. and Douglas A. Shackelford (1998), "State and provincial corporate tax planning: income shifting and sales apportionment factor management, 25 *Journal of Accounting and Economics* 3, pp. 385-406.

Kline, John M. (1983), "The U.S.-U.K. Tax Treaty," in *State Government Influences in U.S. International Economic Policy*, Lexington Books, pp. 127-55.

Kolmar, M. and Andreas Wagener (2004), "The Role of the Tax Base in Tax Competition with Formula Apportionment," University of Vienna, mimeo.

Kroppen, Heinz-Klaus (2004), "Is Europe One Market? A Transfer Pricing Economic Analysis of Pan-European Comparables Sets," Deloitte White Paper background document, EU Joint Transfer Pricing Forum, Brussels, 24 February 2004.

Langbein, Stanley (1986), "The Unitary Method and the Myth of Arm's Length," 30 *Tax Notes* 7 (Feb. 17, 1986), pp. 625-54.

Manzon, Gil B., Jr., and George A. Plesko (2002), "The Relation Between Financial and Tax Reporting Measures of Income," 55 *Tax Law Review* 175, pp. 175-214.

Martin, Philip (2004), "The Day After Tomorrow: The U.K. System After Marks & Spencer," 13 *Tax Management Transfer Pricing Report* 3 (9 June 2004), pp. 117-121.

McDaniel, Paul R. (1994), "Formulary Taxation in the North American Free Trade Zone," 49 *Tax Law Review* 4, pp. 691-744.

McLure, Charles E., Jr. (2002), "Replacing Separate Entity Accounting and the Arm's Length Principle with Formulary Apportionment," 56 *Bulletin for International Fiscal Documentation*, 12 (December), pp. 586-99.

_____ (1981), "The Elusive Incidence of the Corporate Income Tax: The State Case," 9 *Public Finance Quarterly*, pp. 395-413.

_____ (1980), "The State Corporate Income Tax: Lambs in Wolves' Clothing," in Henry S. Aaron and Michael J. Boskin (Eds.) *The Economics of Taxation*, Washington, D.C.: The Brookings Institution, pp. 89-124.

_____ and Joann M. Weiner (2000), "Deciding whether the European Union should adopt Formula Apportionment of Company Income," in Sijbren Cnossen (ed.) *Taxing Capital Income in the European Union. Issues and Options for Reform*, Oxford: Oxford University Press, pp. 243-292.

Meyer, Georganna and Ann Oshiro (1996), "Results of Arizona's Change to a Double-Weighted Sales Factor," 11 *State Tax Notes* 1699 (Dec. 9, 1996), pp. 1699-1703.

Mieszkowski, Peter and George R. Zodrow (1985), "The Incidence of a Partial State Corporate Income Tax," 38 *National Tax Journal* 4, pp. 489-496.

_____ and John Morgan (1984), "The National Effects of Differential State Corporate Income Taxes on Multistate Corporations," in Charles E. McLure, Jr., (ed)., *The State Corporation Income Tax: Issues in Worldwide Unitary Taxation*, Stanford, CA: Hoover Institution Press, pp. 253-263.

Miller, Benjamin F. (1995), "States' Approaches to Combination of Dissimilar Businesses," *State Tax Notes* (June 19, 1995), pp. 2483-2488

_____ (1984), "Worldwide Unitary Combination: The California Practice," in Charles E. McLure, Jr., (ed), *The State Corporation Income Tax: Issues in Worldwide Unitary Taxation*, Stanford, CA: Hoover Institution Press, pp. 132-166.

Mills, Lillian F., Merle M. Erickson, and Edward L. Maydew (1998), "Investments in Tax Planning," 20 *Journal of the American Taxation Association* 1 (Spring 1998), pp. 1-20.

Minnesota Department of Revenue (1993), "Who Pays Minnesota's Household and Business Taxes?" 5 *State Tax Notes* 1483 (Dec. 20, 1993).

Mintz, Jack (2004), "Corporate Tax Harmonization in Europe: It's All About Compliance," 11 *Journal of International Tax and Public Finance* 2 (March), pp. 221-34.

_____ (2002), "European company tax reform: prospects for the future," Vol. 3 CESifo *Forum*, No. 1, (Spring 2002), pp. 3-9.

_____ (2000), "Globalization of the Corporate Income Tax: The Role of Allocation," 56 *Finanzarchiv 3-4,* pp. 389-423.

_____ and Michael Smart (2004), "Income shifting, investment, and tax competition: Theory and evidence from provincial taxation in Canada," 88 *Journal of Public Economics* 6, pp. 1149-68

_____ and Joann M. Weiner (2003), "Exploring Formula Allocation for the European Union," 10 *International Tax and Public Finance* No. 6 (November 2003), pp. 695-711.

Multistate Tax Commission (2003), *Model Regulations, Statutes and Guidelines. Uniformity Recommendations to the States*, Washington, D.C.: Multistate Tax Commission. See http://www.mtc.gov/uniform for the latest updates.

Munnell, Alicia H. (1992), "Taxation of Capital Income in a Global Economy: An Overview," *New England Economic Review* (September/October 1992), pp. 33-52.

Musgrave, Peggy B. (2000), "Interjurisdictional Equity in Company Taxation: Principles and Applications to the European Union," in Sijbren Cnossen (ed.) *Taxing Capital Income in the European Union. Issues and Options for Reform*, Oxford: Oxford University Press, pp. 46-77.

_____(1984), "Principles for Dividing the State Corporate Tax Base," in *The State Corporation Income Tax: Issues in Worldwide Unitary Taxation.* Charles E. McLure, Jr., (ed.), Stanford: Hoover Institution Press, pp. 228-246.

_____(1972), "International Tax Base Division and the Multinational Corporation," 27 *Public Finance* No. 4 pp. 394-413

Nelson, Susan (1999), "Issues in Simplifying the Taxation of Small Business," *Proceedings of the 92nd Annual Conference of the National Tax Association,* pp. 103-113.

Newlon, T. Scott (2000), "Transfer Pricing and Income Shifting in Integrating Economies," in *Taxing Capital Income in the European Union. Issues and Options for Reform*, in Sijbren Cnossen (ed.) Oxford: Oxford University Press, pp. 214-242.46.-77.

Nielsen, Søren Bo, Pascalis Raimondos-Møller, and Guttorm Schjelderup (2004), "Tax Spillovers under Separate Accounting and Formula Apportionment," Economic Policy Research Union paper 01-07, Copenhagen Business School.

Omer, Thomas C. and Marjorie K. Shelley (2004),"Competitive, Political, and Economic Factors Influencing State Tax Policy Changes," *Journal of the American Taxation Association 26 (Supplement)*, pp. 103-126.

Organization for Economic Cooperation and Development (2005), *Model Tax Convention on Income and Capital*, Paris: OECD.

_____ (2004a), "Discussion Draft on the Attribution of Profits to Permanent Establishments. Part I (General Considerations)" Paris: OECD.

_____ (2004b), *Tax Administration in OECD Countries: Comparative Information Series*, OECD, Centre for Tax Policy and Administration, Paris: OECD.

_____ (2003a), "Are the current treaty rules for taxing business profits appropriate for E-commerce?" Public Discussion Draft, 26 November 2003.

_____ (2003b), *Structural Statistics for Industry and Services, 1993-2000,* Paris: OECD.

_____ (1995), *Transfer Pricing Guidelines for Multinational Enterprises and Tax Administrations*, Paris: OECD.

_____ (2000), *Towards Global Tax Co-Operation. Progress in Identifying and Eliminating Harmful Tax Practices,* Paris: OECD.

_____ (1998), *Harmful Tax Competition: An Emerging Global Issue*, Paris: OECD.

Perry, J. Harvey (1989), *A Fiscal History of Canada – The Postwar Years*, Canadian Tax Paper No. 85, Ontario: The Canadian Tax Foundation.

Pethig, Rudiger and Andreas Wagener (2004), "Profit Tax Competition and Formula Apportionment," paper presented at the IIPF conference, Prague.

Plesko, George A. (2002), "Reconciling Corporation Book and Tax Net Income, Tax Years 1996-1998," *Statistics of Income Bulletin*, pp. 111-132.

Przysuski, Martin and Srini Lalapet (2005), "Ontario May Begin International, Interprovincial Transfer Pricing Audits," 39 Tax Notes Int'l 783 (Aug. 29, 2005).

Raventós-Calvo, Stella and José Luis de Juan y Peñalosa (2002), "The Commission's Proposals on Company Taxation from a Spanish Perspective," 42 *European Taxation* 8, pp. 331-335.

Resch, Richard X. (2003), "The Taxation of Profits without a Permanent Establishment," in *Permanent Establishments in International Tax Law*, ed. Hans-Jorgen Aigner and Mario Zuger, Vienna: Linde Vberlag Wien, pp. 475-500.

Robinson, Peyton H. (2000), "The Globally Integrated Multinational, The Arm's-Length Standard, and the Continuum Price Problem," 9 *Tax Management Transfer Pricing. No. 13 Special Report*, Washington, D.C.: Bureau of National Affairs, pp. S3-S24.

Rosenbloom, H. David (2005), "Angel's on a Pin: Arm's Length in the World," 38 *Tax Notes International 523* (9 May 2005), pp. 523-530.

Schoettle, Ferdinand P. (1977), "The U.K. Treaty and the State Taxation of Corporate Income," 5 *Tax Notes* 3 (Apr. 4, 1977).

Shay, Stephen E., J. Clifton Fleming, Jr., and Robert J. Peroni (2002), "What's source got to do with it? Source rules and U.S. international taxation," 56 *Tax Law Review* No. 1, pp. 81-156.

Sheffrin, Steve M. and Jack Fulcher (1984), "Alternative divisions of the tax base: How much is at stake?' in Charles E. McLure, Jr. (ed.), *The State Corporation Income Tax: Issues in Worldwide Unitary Combination*, Stanford, CA: Hoover Institution Press, pp. 192-213.

Sheppard, Lee (2005), "Dowdy Retailer Set to Destroy European Corporate Tax, Part 2," 38 *Tax Notes Int'l* 627 (23 May 2005).

Shipley, David J., Scott D. Smith, and Brad A. Bauer (2004), "A New Paradigm for State Corporate Income Tax Planning: Part I --- The Changing State Environment," 33 *State Tax Notes* (September 6, 2004), pp. 707-22.

Smith, Ernest H. (1998), *Federal-Provincial Tax Sharing and Centralized Tax Collection in Canada*, Special Studies in Taxation and Public Finance, No. 1, Canadian Tax Foundation.

_____ (1976), "Allocating to provinces the taxable income of corporations: How the federal-provincial allocation rules evolved," *Canadian Tax Journal*, Vol. 24, pp. 545-71.

Sorensen, Peter B. (2004), "Company tax reform in the European Union," 11 *Journal of International Tax and Public Finance* 1, pp. 91-115.

Summers, Lawrence H. (1988),"Taxation in a Small World," in *Tax Policy in the Twenty-First Century* Herbert Stein (ed.), New York: John Wiley & Sons, pp. 64-75.

Tax Analysts (2002), "e-Forum: Company Taxation in the European Union," 25 *Tax Notes International* 153 (January 14, 2002), pp. 153-174.

Treff, Karen and David B. Perry (2003), *Finances of the Nation. A review of the expenditures and revenues of the federal, provincial, and local governments of Canada,* Ontario: Canadian Tax Foundation.

Union of Industrial and Employers' Confederations of Europe (UNICE) (2004), *Letter to Commissioner Frits Bolkestein from UNICE Secretary General*, 6 September 2004.

_____ (2000), "Memorandum on cross-border company taxation obstacles in the Single Market," April 2000.

_____ (1999), "Transfer Pricing Issues and the Arbitration Convention," joint UNICE/European Round Table memo, September 1999.

_____ (1994), "Letter from UNICE Secretary General Zygmunt Tyszkiewicz to U.S. Treasury Assistant Secretary Leslie B. Samuels," 26 January 1994.

Unilever (2004), *Annual Report.*

UK Inland Revenue (2005), *International Manual* (INTM460150), United Kingdom.

U.S. Department of the Treasury (2000), *The Deferral of Income Earned Through U.S. Controlled Foreign Corporations. A Policy Study*, Washington, D.C.: U.S. Treasury, Office of Tax Policy.

\-\-\-\-\- (1996), *Conference on Formula Apportionment*, December 12, 1996, Office of Tax Policy, Washington, D.C.

\-\-\-\-\- and the Internal Revenue Service (1988), "A Study of Intercompany Pricing Under Section 482 of the Code (the White Paper)," Notice 88-123, 1988-2 C.B. 458.

U.S. General Accounting Office (1995), *California Taxes on Multinational Corporations and Related Federal Issues*, GAO/GGD-95-171, Washington, D.C.

U.S. House of Representatives (1964), *Report of the Special Subcommittee on State Taxation, 1: State taxation of interstate commerce* (the Willis Report), 88th Congress, 2nd Session, Washington, D.C.: U.S. Government Printing Office.

Vanistendael, Frans (1992), "Comments on the Ruding Committee Report," *EC Tax Review*, 1.

Weiner, Joann Martens (2005), "Formulary Apportionment and Group Taxation in the European Union: Insights from the United States and Canada," *European Commission Taxation Working Paper* No. 8, Luxembourg: Commission of the European Communities.

_____ (2001a), "The European Union and Formula Apportionment: Caveat Emptor," 41 *European Taxation 10* (October), pp. 380-88.

_____ (2001b), "EU Commission Study on Company Taxation and the Internal Market Considers Comprehensive Company Tax Reform," 24 *Tax Notes International* 511 (October 29, 2001), pp. 511-18.

_____ (1999), "Using the Experience in the U.S. States to Evaluate Issues in Implementing Formula Apportionment at the International Level," OTA Paper 83, Office of Tax Analysis, Washington, D.C.: U.S. Department of the Treasury.

_____ (1994), *Company Taxation for the European Community. How Sub-National Tax Variation Affects Business Investment in the United States and Canada*, Harvard University Ph.D. dissertation (unpublished).

_____ (1992), "Tax coordination and competition in the United States of America," Annex 9C in *Report of the Committee of Independent Experts on Company Taxation (the Ruding Report)*, Luxembourg: Official Publications of the European Communities, pp. 417-38.

Wellisch, Dietmar (2004), "Taxation under formula apportionment --- tax competition, tax incidence, and the choice of apportionment factors," 60 *Finanzarchiv* 1, pp. 24-41.

Westberg, Björn (2002) "Consolidated Corporate Tax Bases for EU-Wide Activities: Evaluation of Four Proposals Presented by the European Commission," 42 *European Taxation* 8, pp. 322-30.

Wetzler, James W. (1995), "Should the U.S. Adopt Formula Apportionment?" 48 *National Tax Journal* 3, pp. 357-62.

Wilson, John D. (1999), "Theories of Tax Competition," 52 *National Tax Journal* 2, pp. 269-304.

INDEX

Advantages of formulary apportionment, 40–41
Alabama
  passive investment company legislation, 84
  state apportionment tax rate, 91
Alaska
  mandatory combined reporting, 84
  state apportionment tax rate, 91
Alberta, apportionment calculation, 56
AMID case, cross border losses, 27
Apportionment calculation, Canada, 56
Apportionment factor definitions, locations
  Canadian provinces, 54
  locations of factors, 51–54
Apportionment formula, 47–60
  Canada, 54–55
    apportionment calculation in, 56
  definitions, 51–54
  formulary apportionment
    factor weights, choosing, 50
    practice, choosing factors in, 49–50
    preliminary issues, 48–49
    principles of, 48–50
    theory, choosing factors in, 49
  industries, formulae for, 55–57
  payroll, 52–53
  property, 52
  sales, 53–54
  state apportionment formula, illustration of, 55
  Uniform Division of Income for Tax Purposes Act, 51
  United States states, 54
Arizona

  mandatory combined reporting, 84
  state apportionment tax rate, 91
Arkansas
  passive investment company legislation, 84
  state apportionment tax rate, 91
Athinaiki case, tax on distribution deemed withholding tax, 27
Austria
  corporate income tax rate, 19
  domestic, cross-border loss offsetting, 20
  employee distribution, 38
  EU tax rate, 94
Avoir Fiscal case, imputation tax credit, 27

Bachmann case, taxation of workers, 27
Barclays Bank case, 6
Belgium
  corporate income tax rate, 19
  domestic, cross-border loss offsetting, 20
  employee distribution, 38
  EU tax rate, 94
Bosal Holding BV case, 27
British Columbia, apportionment calculation, 56
Business income, 66

Cadbury Schweppes case, 27
California
  mandatory combined reporting, 84
  state apportionment tax rate, 91
Canada, 69–70
  apportionment calculation in, 56
  apportionment formula, 54–55

CCCTB WG. *See* Common Consolidated
    Corporate Tax Base Working Group
Colorado
    mandatory combined reporting, 84
    state apportionment tax rate, 91
Commission v. Belgium case, deductibility
    of insurance payments, 27
Commission v. France (Avoir Fiscal) case,
    imputation tax credit, 27
Common Consolidated Corporate Tax Base
    Working Group, 29, 33
    European Commission, 64
Company tax reform, 1–15, 17–32
Compliance costs, 79–80
Compliance issues, 77–88
Connecticut
    passive investment company legislation,
        84
    state apportionment tax rate, 91
Consolidation, 70
Corporate income tax rates, EU-15, EU
    member states, 19
COST. *See* Council on State Taxation
Council on State Taxation, 78–79
Cross-border income shifting, 23
Cross-border loss compensation, 18–20
Cross-border tax, 18–25
Cyprus
    corporate income tax rate, 19
    domestic, cross-border loss offsetting, 20
    employee distribution, 38
    EU tax rate, 94
Czech Rep.
    domestic, cross-border loss offsetting, 20
    EU tax rate, 94
Czech Republic
    corporate income tax rate, 19
    employee distribution, 38

Definitions, apportionment formula, 51–54
Delaware, state apportionment tax rate, 91
Denmark
    corporate income tax rate, 19
    domestic, cross-border loss offsetting, 20
    employee distribution, 38
    EU tax rate, 94
Disadvantages of formulary apportionment,
    41–44
District of Columbia, state apportionment
    tax rate, 91
Domestic
    cross-border, loss offsetting, EU member
        states, 20

    cross-border loss offsetting, EU member
        states, 20

Economic presence, taxable connections,
    62–63
Employee distribution, EU member states, 38
Employment, 96–97
Employment shares, potential income
    distribution using, 37–38
Estonia
    corporate income tax rate, 19
    domestic, cross-border loss offsetting, 20
    employee distribution, 38
    EU tax rate, 94
European Commission, 1–3
    strategy of, 1–3
European Court of Justice
    direct tax cases, 27
    influences from, 26–29
European multinational enterprise, 38–40

Factor weights, choosing, formulary
    apportionment, 50
Federation of Tax Administrators, 78–79
Finland
    corporate income tax rate, 19
    domestic, cross-border loss offsetting, 20
    employee distribution, 38
    EU tax rate, 94
Fiscal externalities, 100–102
Florida, state apportionment tax rate, 91
Foreign direct investment, taxation, 17–18
Formulary apportionment, 1–15, 33–46
    advantages of, 40–41
    Common Consolidated Corporate Tax
        Base Working Group, 33
    common formula, tax base, empirical
        evidence, 97–98
    different formulae, revenue effects under,
        98–99
    disadvantages of, 41–44
    economic analysis, 89–104
    employee distribution, EU member states,
        38
    employment, 96–97
    employment shares, potential income
        distribution using, 37–38
    European multinational enterprise, 38–40
    factor choices, impact on, 95–96
    fiscal externalities, 100–102
    illustrations, 34–37
        European union data, 37–40
    implementation of, 105–107

income distribution under, 35
investment, 96–97
marginal effective tax rates, derivation,
    under apportionment, 93
Minnesota Department of Revenue,
    incidence of state corporate income
    tax, 89
obstacles to, 5–7
overview of, 33–37
provincial profits formula, 34
sales effects, 96–97
in single market, 7–9
state apportionment tax rates, 91
state profits formula, 34
tax competition, 100–102
technical analysis, 89–95
theoretical analysis of, 99–102
France
    corporate income tax rate, 19
    domestic, cross-border loss offsetting, 20
    employee distribution, 38
    EU tax rate, 94
FTA. *See* Federation of Tax Administrators
Futura Participations case, cross-border
    loss compensation, 27

*Geoffrey, Inc. v. South Carolina Tax
    Commission* case, 62–63
    Delaware Corporation, 62
Georgia
    passive investment company legislation,
        84
    state apportionment tax rate, 91
Germany
    corporate income tax rate, 19
    domestic, cross-border loss offsetting, 20
    employee distribution, 38
    EU tax rate, 94
Governmental responses, 83–84
Governments of EU, 20–24
Greece
    corporate income tax rate, 19
    domestic, cross-border loss offsetting, 20
    employee distribution, 38
    EU tax rate, 94

Hawaii
    mandatory combined reporting, 84
    state apportionment tax rate, 91
Hoechst case, advance corporation tax, 27
Hungary
    corporate income tax rate, 19
    domestic, cross-border loss offsetting, 20

employee distribution, 38
EU tax rate, 94

ICI v. Colmer case, group/consortium relief,
    27
Idaho
    mandatory combined reporting, 84
    state apportionment tax rate, 91
Illinois
    mandatory combined reporting, 84
    state apportionment tax rate, 91
Illustrations of formulary apportionment,
    34–37
    European union data, 37–40
Income distribution under formulary
    apportionment, 35
Income shifting
    cross-border, 23
    evidence of, 24–25
Income tax rates, corporate, EU-15, EU
    member states, 19
Indiana, state apportionment tax rate, 91
Industries, formulae for, 55–57
Investment, 96–97
Iowa, state apportionment tax rate, 91
Ireland
    corporate income tax rate, 19
    domestic, cross-border loss offsetting, 20
    employee distribution, 38
    EU tax rate, 94
Italy
    corporate income tax rate, 19
    domestic, cross-border loss offsetting, 20
    employee distribution, 38
    EU tax rate, 94

Kansas
    mandatory combined reporting, 84
    state apportionment tax rate, 91
Kentucky
    passive investment company legislation,
        84
    state apportionment tax rate, 91

Labrador, apportionment calculation, 56
Lankhorst-Hohorst case, 27, 29
Lasertec case, 27
Latvia
    corporate income tax rate, 19
    domestic, cross-border loss offsetting, 20
    employee distribution, 38
    EU tax rate, 94
Lenz case, foreign dividends, 27

Leur-Bloem case, tax avoidance, 27
Lithuania
    corporate income tax rate, 19
    domestic, cross-border loss offsetting, 20
    employee distribution, 38
    EU tax rate, 94
Louisiana, state apportionment tax rate, 91
Luxembourg
    corporate income tax rate, 19
    domestic, cross-border loss offsetting, 20
    employee distribution, 38

Maine
    mandatory combined reporting, 84
    state apportionment tax rate, 91
Malta
    corporate income tax rate, 19
    domestic, cross-border loss offsetting, 20
    employee distribution, 38
Manitoba, apportionment calculation, 56
Manninen case, cross-border dividend
    imputation credit, 27
Marginal effective tax rates, derivation,
    under apportionment, 93
Marks Spencer case, 27–28
Maryland
    passive investment company legislation,
        84
    state apportionment tax rate, 91
Massachusetts
    passive investment company legislation,
        84
    state apportionment tax rate, 91
Metallgesellschaft case, taxation of group
    income, 27
Minnesota
    mandatory combined reporting, 84
    state apportionment tax rate, 91
Minnesota Department of Revenue,
    incidence of state corporate income tax,
        89
Mississippi
    passive investment company legislation,
        84
    state apportionment tax rate, 91
Missouri, state apportionment tax rate, 91
Model Income Tax Convention, OECD, 4
Montana
    mandatory combined reporting, 84
    state apportionment tax rate, 91
MTC. *See* Multistate Tax Commission
Multinational taxation, 3–4

Multistate businesses, state tax authorities,
    cooperation, 78–79
Multistate corporation, computation of state
    taxable income, 67
Multistate Tax Commission, 78–79
Multistate tax organizations, 78–79
    United States, 78–79

Nebraska
    mandatory combined reporting, 84
    state apportionment tax rate, 91
Netherlands
    corporate income tax rate, 19
    domestic, cross-border loss offsetting, 20
    employee distribution, 38
    EU tax rate, 94
New Brunswick, apportionment calculation,
    56
New Hampshire
    mandatory combined reporting, 84
    state apportionment tax rate, 91
New Jersey
    passive investment company legislation,
        84
    state apportionment tax rate, 91
New Mexico, state apportionment tax rate,
    91
New York
    passive investment company legislation,
        84
    state apportionment tax rate, 91
Newfoundland, apportionment calculation,
    56
Nexus. *See* Taxable connections
Non-business income, tax base, 66
North Carolina
    passive investment company legislation,
        84
    state apportionment tax rate, 91
North Dakota
    mandatory combined reporting, 84
    state apportionment tax rate, 91
Northwest Territories, apportionment
    calculation, 56
Nova Scotia, apportionment calculation, 56
Nunavut, apportionment calculation, 56

OECD Model Income Tax Convention, 4
Ohio
    passive investment company legislation,
        84
    state apportionment tax rate, 91
Oklahoma, state apportionment tax rate, 91

Ontario, apportionment calculation, 56
Oregon
    mandatory combined reporting, 84
    state apportionment tax rate, 91
Overview of formulary apportionment,
    33–37

Passive investment companies, tax planning,
    82
Payroll, apportionment formula, 52–53
Pennsylvania, state apportionment tax rate,
    91
Permanent establishment, taxable
    connections, 63–64
Physical presence, taxable connections, 62
Poland
    corporate income tax rate, 19
    domestic, cross-border loss offsetting, 20
    employee distribution, 38
    EU tax rate, 94
Portugal
    corporate income tax rate, 19
    domestic, cross-border loss offsetting, 20
    employee distribution, 38
    EU tax rate, 94
Practice, choosing factors in, formulary
    apportionment, 49–50
Preliminary issues, formulary
    apportionment, 48–49
Prince Edward Island, apportionment
    calculation, 56
Principles of formulary apportionment,
    48–50
Property, apportionment formula, 52
Provincial profits formula, formulary
    apportionment, 34
Provincial taxable income, 67–68

Quebec, apportionment calculation, 56
Quill Corp. v. North Dakota case, 62–63

Rhode Island, state apportionment tax rate,
    91

Saint-Gobain case, treatment of branches, 27
Sales, apportionment formula, 53–54
Sales effects, 96–97
Saskatchewan, apportionment calculation, 56
Schmacker case, taxation of workers, 27
SEA. See Single European Act
Single European Act, 25
Single market creation in EU, 25–26
Slovakia

corporate income tax rate, 19
domestic, cross-border loss offsetting, 20
employee distribution, 38
EU tax rate, 94
Slovenia
    corporate income tax rate, 19
    domestic, cross-border loss offsetting, 20
    employee distribution, 38
    EU tax rate, 94
South Carolina, state apportionment tax rate,
    91
Spain
    corporate income tax rate, 19
    domestic, cross-border loss offsetting, 20
    employee distribution, 38
    EU tax rate, 94
State apportionment formula, illustration of,
    55
State apportionment tax rates, 91
State corporate income tax, mechanics of,
    66–67
State profits formula, formulary
    apportionment, 34
State tax authorities, multistate businesses
    cooperation, 78–79
Strategy of European Commission, 1–3
Sweden
    corporate income tax rate, 19
    domestic, cross-border loss offsetting, 20
    employee distribution, 38
    EU tax rate, 94

Tax administration, 77–88
Tax base, 64–68
    business income, 66
    Common Consolidated Corporate Tax
        Base Working Group, European
        Commission, 64
    multistate corporation, computation of
        state taxable income, 67
    non-business income, 66
    provincial taxable income, 67–68
    state corporate income tax, mechanics of,
        66–67
    United States, state taxable income, 65–66
Tax competition, 100–102
Tax planning, 77–88
    factor shifting, 81–82
    passive investment companies, 82
    water's edge reporting, 84–86
Taxable connections, 62–64
    economic presence, 62–63
    intangible presence, 62–63

permanent establishment, 63–64
physical presence, 62
treaty-based substantial presence tests, 64
Taxable unit, 68–72
   Canada, 69–70
   consolidation, 70
   unitary combined reporting, 70–72
   water's edge consolidation, 70
   worldwide consolidation, 70
Tennessee, state apportionment tax rate, 91
Theory, choosing factors in, formulary
   apportionment, 49
Transfer pricing documentation
   requirements, 20–22
Treaty-based substantial presence tests,
   taxable connections, 64
Treaty of Rome, 17, 25

UDITPA. See Uniform Division of Income
   for Tax Purposes Act
UNICF. See Union of Industrial and
   Employers' Confederation in Europe
Uniform Division of Income for Tax
   Purposes Act, 51
Union of Industrial and Employers'
   Confederation in Europe, 2
Unitary combined reporting, 70–72
United Kingdom
   corporate income tax rate, 19
   domestic, cross-border loss offsetting, 20

employee distribution, 38
EU tax rate, 94
United States
   multistate tax organizations, 78–79
   state taxable income, 65–66
United States states, 54
Utah
   mandatory combined reporting, 84
   state apportionment tax rate, 91

Verkooijen case, dividend exemption, 27
Vermont
   mandatory combined reporting, 84
   state apportionment tax rate, 91
Virginia
   passive investment company legislation,
      84
   state apportionment tax rate, 91

Water's edge consolidation, 70
Water's edge reporting, 84–86
West Virginia, state apportionment tax rate,
   91
Wisconsin, state apportionment tax rate, 91
Worldwide consolidation, 70

X AB and Y AB case, domestic losses, 27

Yukon, apportionment calculation, 56